Turn Off the Noise and Invest Now

A Guide to Understanding Investments and Preparing for Your Financial Future

Sean D. Castle

with T. L. Heyer

D1572640

WordServe Press
Centennial, Colo.

Invest Now

WordServe Press, a division of WordServe Literary, 7500 E. Arapahoe Rd. Suite 285, Centennial, CO 80112 admin@wordserveliterary.com, 303.471.6675

All permissions inquiries should be addressed to the address above.

Cover Design: U.T Dezines
Interior Book Design: Greg Johnson

Ordering Information: Quantity sales: Special discounts are available on quantity purchases by corporations, associations, and others. For details, contact "Admin" at the email address or phone number above.

Sean Castle, 1965
First Edition: December 2022
ISBN: 978-1-941555-56-9
Printed in the United States of America

Turn Off the Noise and Invest Now

Invest Now

TABLE OF CONTENTS

INTRODUCTION

Imagine the last time you were on an airplane. My wife and I travel quite a bit, and I imagine you follow a similar routine every time, like we do. You know the drill. You board the plane, you find your seat, you stow your luggage above, and you settle in with your books and snacks. (I do hope you're not one of those people who buys garlic-infused sushi to stink up the plane.)

Just before takeoff, the flight attendants take their places in the aisle to tell us everything we need to do regarding cabin safety in the event of an emergency. We're all supposed to watch the demonstration to learn where the exits are, how to buckle our seatbelts, where to find oxygen masks and life vests, and not to smoke on the plane. Some airlines require the flight attendants to follow a script, and others let them be creative with their own shtick. Either way, formal or funny, the flight attendant becomes the guide for the journey.

You have probably noticed, as I have, that people respond differently to flight attendants and their instructions.

Some people don't pay any attention to the spiel and the speech. They've flown so many times that this announcement is background noise, as invisible as the purr of the engine. They don't fold up their newspapers or turn off their tablets. They're trusting the captain and crew to get them safely to their destination, and they're not worried. Could they reach their destination without instructions? Likely. They're willing to let someone else be in charge.

Other passengers sit up straight and tall, attentive like they're in the front row of a lecture hall. They take notes as if there will be a quiz. They want to know what to do and how to respond, should there be anything unexpected on this flight. Will they benefit from paying careful attention? Perhaps. If the plane hits some turbulence, we're all going to be thankful someone paid attention.

Perhaps this book is the beginning of a journey for you. Maybe you've come into some money, and you're wondering how to make it grow or last. Maybe you have landed your first salaried position as a young adult, an inheritance in your midlife, or a 401(k) at the brink of your retirement. You have started on a journey of understanding your investments, and now you're wondering how to navigate this path. Let's talk about it.

Could you travel each of these journeys without a guide? Probably. But if things get rough ahead, you're going to be thankful someone paid attention.

Retirement Planning is No Longer Attached to a Certain Age

Fifty years ago, it was common that people worked decades for the same company, forever paying into a pension and retirement plan that they could receive after a finish-line retirement party. But that is rarely the case anymore. Many a fifty-something sees retirement coming straight at them, and they don't have a plan.

On the flipside, we used to assume that investors in their thirties had a small amount to set aside, but that's not true anymore either. Many a young investor has had a windfall with financial fortune and technology success in their early years. The former age-appropriate financial advice is not as applicable as it used to be, and it's not as clear cut as it once was. People are retiring later, and they're getting rich younger.

So, rather than starting with an age-related approach, let's talk about your experience with financial planning.

This Book is for the Person Who is Just Getting Started

I don't believe in intimidation tactics or a business model of talking over people's heads. I have written this book for the novice, and my desire is to keep it simple and equip you with the conversational tools to help you feel comfortable navigating your money. We will not get into the nitty-gritty of investing, and I'm not going to talk about trading techniques, day trading, or all the fancy stuff of the trading floor. Our conversations in these pages will scratch the surface, giving you some ideas, vocabulary, and confidence.

I have been managing money since 1987, and I founded a successful investment company in Denver, Colorado in 1994.

After thirty years in the financial industry, you could say I've flown this flight a few times. I've been down this road before. I've helped families, couples, and individuals of any age to understand the ups and downs, the range of emotions, and ultimately the psychology of investing. I have learned to recognize the common obstacles that trip people up, and I can see what you are up against. I'd like to teach you the necessary terms and concepts to get you investing, saving for retirement, and the truth of whether it's possible to save too much.

To start, we will look at the psychology of investing, specifically the tendency toward rollercoaster emotions that go up and down with the market. I will show you how to navigate that path by knowing what you're up against. We will compare Wall Street to Your Street—two very different places that are not equally safe for you and your interests. We will identify what— and who—will make your money work for you, what sources you can trust, which ones are not helpful at all, and what pitfalls you should avoid from the very beginning.

In the next section, we will talk about investing tools by explaining the important terms like stocks and bonds, mutual funds and ETFs – the nuts and bolts of information you need to start investing. We will look at how to get started, where to begin, and—one of the most powerful tools of investing—the power of compound interest.

To close out the book, we will talk about achieving your goals for retirement. While life's situations and seasons may shift, the end goals usually stay the same: financial independence and freedom in your later years. Most people are investing for retirement, so we will talk about what to do when you get there.

As I said, could you navigate this on your own? Perhaps. Maybe the answer is even "probably."

My goal for this book is to provide you with a foundation to begin your journey. I want you to learn and understand the basics. I want you to understand what's happening here. In fact, I want everyone to understand what we're doing.

I've got a map, and I can show you a path to get you on the right track. My goal is not to be the pilot of your plane, but the guide for your path.

You can start small, and you can start today. Let's go, shall we?

CHAPTER ONE

The Most Important Rule . . .
Turn Off the Noise

"The only value of stock forecasters is to make fortune tellers look good." --Warren Buffett

Any trustworthy guide will begin by telling you the most important safety rule for the journey.

If you're white-water rafting, the guide will tell you to always wear your life jacket and do your best to stay in the boat. If you're hiking, the guide will tell you to stay with the group and know the forecasted weather conditions. If you're on a bicycle tour, the guide will tell you to go with the traffic flow and to wear your helmet. If you're taking a cooking class, the guide will make sure you know where the fire extinguisher is. On any journey, we want to know what could go wrong and how we can avoid it.

There is a psychology of danger. In the face of risk, we are hardwired with instincts to protect ourselves and the ones we love most, and that response is consistent whether the danger is real or only perceived. We fully intend to do what must be done to save ourselves and the people in our lives, but we make mistakes when we are scared. That's why it is best to have a plan in place with steps to follow before things go south. It is the guide's job to give appropriate levels of information, so you don't panic in the face of hard decisions.

But imagine this.

What if the travel industry had someone hiding behind the scenes, stirring the pot and messing with your psychology, aiming to create panic and despair on a regular basis? What if they could somehow equip you with an earpiece that whispered to you the worst scenarios that could go wrong? What if they could interrupt your journey with forecasts and hypotheticals to perpetuate your anxiety? Worse yet, what if that industry were *making money* every time you reacted?

You and I could both conclude that their instructions would not be in our best interests. If someone benefits in any way from your worry, fear, and anxiety, that person is not our ally. And yet, these fear mongers are often the ones trying to hijack our attention.

Today's news headlines are designed to generate as many views and clicks as possible, and they do that by exploiting our fears. They are manipulating us to believe we are in danger.

(You might want to sit down before I say this, just in case you're someone who reads a book while standing.)

7

Invest Now

When it comes to the journey of managing your money, there are people behind the scenes who are messing with our minds, hoping we will get scared and follow their bad advice. And worse yet, there is someone *making money* every time we give in to the panic and make dramatic changes in our investments.

Noisy Headlines are Not in Our Favor

Somewhere, in a world not far away, someone is making money because they wrote a good headline that made us gasp, click, take action, and look for guidance to "protect" ourselves and our families. And that headline may – *or may not* – be true. Most often, there's actually nothing to worry about. It's just a misleading hook to get our attention.

I wrote for financial business newsletters early in my career, and I can tell you that fear sells. Why is that? Because we are less likely to buy a newsletter or click on a headline if the sales pitch says all is calm and the future is bright. But if they can get us to buy into the fear of financial dangers lurking around every corner, they'll grab our attention and possibly scare us into becoming their subscribers. If we have given them a voice in our lives – on our internet browsers or in the morning news clips – then we are already at their mercy. They are painting worst-case scenarios to manipulate our decisions and get us to purchase their products.

I've watched those guys on the morning news while I am getting ready for work, and so many of them are outside their wheelhouse of expertise. Their specialty is TV news and morning traffic, not financial markets. Whenever there is a big up or down day in the market, they create panic that they can't really justify. The morning craziness—a cycle of fearful buying and selling—perpetuates old drama that we become addicted to, and I think it's fair to say that our entire population is addicted to the dopamine rush of panic and drama. I call it Panic Porn.

If we allow ourselves to become pawns in the game of Panic Porn, we will freak out three or four times a year, right when the media wants us to. We will buy and sell, buy and sell, all on a vicious emotional cycle. Over time, that kind of buying and selling will not only zero out our returns, but it may also cause us to "lock in" our losses. This is the most common mistake of the individual investor. This is not in the best interests of our money, our blood pressure, our day, or our future.

The greatest danger is not the market itself, but allowing others to manipulate and exploit our fears, driving us out of the market completely.

Money worries are common to most of us, whether we're concerned about our retirement accounts or the very present reality of making ends meet this month. Unfortunately, Wall Street fully embraces emotional investors, because that level of emotionality and instability creates more money for them. Market makers and brokerage firms are making money when the media preys on our financial concerns, creating a sense of urgency that triggers an emotional response.

Invest Now

If we look at the trend of headlines in the last decade, most of them seem to threaten recession. But if we look at the trends of the stock market, it has continued to rise in the backdrop of those headlines. No matter which direction the market was headed – most of the time solidly rising or occasionally dipping – the headlines projected endless gloom and doom.

Historical Trends of Major Market Events

When something new is on the horizon, whether it is good news or bad news, people tend to believe it's a ticking bomb that's going to wipe us all out financially. So, the media plays like a beating drum with the same message they want us to hear: *Get Scared! Time to Panic!*

Even when the headlines are right, when the media predicts a fall that actually happens, the market recovers. The economy and the markets are always growing over time. It may go into a recession, but the long-term economic trajectory is always upward.

If we zoom in on the graphs that cover the entire history of the market, we will see bumps along the way, but the market will recover. It always does. Let it run its course.

The Patterns of the Tortoise and the Hare

Years ago, my company managed the retirement funds for a mid-size technology firm. More than fifty people worked for this company, and we offered our services to everyone on their staff –

from the hourly employees to the top-level executives. Here's what I learned from that experience: on occasion, since top-level executives know a lot about one thing, they can sometimes deceive themselves into thinking that they know a lot about everything. In this case, the executives wanted to manage their own money, which certainly everyone has the right to do – whether it is best for them or not.

The executives were buying and trading all the time, making almost-constant changes to their portfolios. They were basically day trading. They were watching the headlines and talking heads, and they were calling my office several times a week to make changes based on the most recent rants of an on-air entertainer playing the role of an investment guru.

Meanwhile, those who were mid-level in the company—we could also affirm them as those who were comfortable following directions—placed their investments carefully and with expert advice.

Then they let their money do what it can do: they let it work for them. Instead of calling me multiple times a week to make changes, they let their money do the slow work of time in the market.

Let me let you in on the spoiler alert: the mid-level employees made excellent returns on their money, while the partners of the tech firm were losing about twenty percent a year. The executives were looking for homeruns instead of base hits. They were looking to beat the system instead of trusting the process. They were chasing the shortcuts of the hare, when the best route is to follow the wisdom of the tortoise.

The Most Important Rule

Just like a trusted guide begins with the important safety tips for the journey, here is the single most important rule I want you to take into the journey ahead of you: Turn off the Noise.

Major network financial news is horrible for the individual investor, because unleashed fear has the power to ruin people's lives. We all make mistakes when we get scared. In his book *Rich Dad, Poor Dad,* Robert Kiyosaki wrote, "Emotions are what make us human. Make us real. The word 'emotion' stands for energy in motion. Be truthful about your emotions, and use your mind and emotions in your favor, not against yourself."[1]

Turn Off the Noise.

There are natural fears when it comes to investing and saving, and there are invented fears based on emotions. There is a reasonable response, and there is an unreasonable response. Natural fears are inherent to the risk involved, but the invented fears are the ones that can drown your financial future.

The Money Guys, Brian Preston and Bo Hanson, wrote, "Overconsumption of financial media in particular can cause what's known as analysis paralysis. . .. Information overload, combined with conflicting views, means you won't have any idea what to do and may be unable to make a decision. It's important to limit your consumption of harmful and fear mongering sources of information because your decision-making skills (and even your happiness) could be negatively impacted."[2]

The Money Guys are right.

Anytime I have a client who watches these channels regularly, I encourage them to sign off. I can tell from our first conversations that they're going to get emotional; they're going to watch the market fluctuate, they're going to get sucked into the machine of Panic Porn, and they're going to want to buy or sell based on their emotions. I've had clients throughout the years who have called me from their living room, crying as they were watching the financial news channel, terrified of what was going to happen next. I don't want that to happen to you. Nobody can function that way. *Turn off the noise.*

When you turn off the noise, you're able to take the emotions out of investing. In fact, if we can teach an individual investor to turn off the noise, we've already helped them to succeed. If you can take the emotionality out of the equation, you've already become a more effective investor.

The key is not timing the market. The key is time in the market.

The key to success is not to move your money around by timing the market. The key to success is to let your money stay the course with time *in* the market.

Don't let anyone's drama fool you. Check your emotions, stick with your plan, and turn off the noise. It's the single most successful thing you can do for your investments.

CHAPTER TWO

Get Started
The Benefits of The Early Start

"A man doesn't plant a tree for himself. He plants it for posterity." --Alexander Smith

We all love a payday. I have the privilege of working with young people who are learning to navigate their brand-new finances, and I have yet to meet one who isn't thrilled with getting paid. There's nothing like receiving your first paycheck because it brings a great degree of freedom for today—and responsibility to save for the future.

A lifetime of paychecks can add up to an impressive amount of money with a significant number of zeroes. As I write this book, the lifetime income of someone with a high school diploma is $1.3 million,[3] Americans with a college degree can plan on earning $2.3 million throughout their lifetime, and those who continue onto graduate school may earn a median of $3.6 million.[4] It sounds like a lot of money when you look at the accumulation

15

over a lifetime, but very few people actually receive one check with that many zeroes. When we stretch it out over a career, considering a life's worth of expenses and how long each of us might live, that large sum breaks down into much smaller chunks.

Still, if it's likely that a million dollars will pass through your hands throughout the course of your lifetime, how can you utilize that money to prepare for the journey ahead? The quick answer is to set aside some of each paycheck as savings for the future. After all, as Robert Kiyosaki wrote, "Most people fail to realize that in life, it's not how much money you make, it's how much money you keep."[5]

Aside from the earned paycheck, sometimes people have what I call Found Money, meaning they have received an unexpected chunk of money. Maybe a grandparent has died, and now they have happened onto an inheritance. Maybe they have a 401(k) they have been paying into for forty years, and suddenly it's in their hands. They want to know how to make the money last, how much they can safely withdraw, and how to make the money work for them. Here are my thoughts.

Start the Plan Today

Start saving money as early as you can – as young as possible. When you invest money on a regular basis, your retirement accounts will add up over time. So, the earlier you start to save, the more your money will grow throughout your lifetime.

On the next page, take a look at this example, Investor A and Investor B. They each begin with the same amount of money, but Investor A starts their retirement savings at age twenty-five, while Investor B begins their investing at age thirty-five. Look what a difference that early start makes, even just by ten years. Although they began with the same amount of money, by age 65, Investor A has almost twice as much wealth as Investor B. Savings and time are key components to financial health. The earlier you begin, the larger your account can grow.

Get Started Today
The Benefits of the Early Start

Pay Yourself First.

If you have ever managed your own finances, then you already know that saving money can be difficult. If it were easy, everyone would do it, but there seems to be an endless stream of expenses that demand a piece of each month's paycheck.

The trick is to prioritize. Put your future first. **When you pay yourself first, you get the cream at the top of the bucket, and not the leftovers at the bottom.** This may require some small lifestyle changes, but as you see your net worth steadily increase, you may find that saving becomes less of short-term challenge and more of an exciting, long-term commitment.

Set aside a portion of money from every paycheck before any of the paycheck is spent. Many people use banks to implement this strategy, and most large employers—and some smaller ones as well—are equipped to send paychecks directly to bank accounts. Some people delineate specific amounts to separate accounts, one for everyday expenses and the other for saving toward a goal.

For example, a person who wants to save $200 from their twice-monthly paycheck of $2000 might ask their employer to send $1800 to their account for daily expenses, and the remaining $200 could be sent to an investment account. Since that money is out of sight, you will not be as tempted to spend it. With this small step, you have paid yourself first. You get a portion of the best, not the rest of what's leftover.

What Will You Do with the Money You Save?

Define Your Goals. Knowing how to secure your financial well-being is one of the most important things you can do for yourself, and your savings is the key to creating the life you want. What do you want to achieve with your investments? I've discovered a few common focus points among the many people I've worked with, and this list may help you define your sense of direction.

Emergency fund. We have all experienced unexpected financial emergencies, and they can pack quite a punch. A leaky roof, a dental bill, a kid's broken leg, an unexpected job lay-off, or even a damaged laptop computer can set you back. Big and small, these hiccups seem to arrive at the worst times. Only four out of ten people have enough cash to cover a $1,000 financial hit.[6] If you have a dedicated emergency fund to protect yourself and your family, you can prepare to recover from these unplanned expenses.

529 Plan

A tax-advantaged savings plan designed to encourage saving for educational expenses. All fifty states sponsor at least one type of 529 plan, and each one is designed to make saving for college much easier.

Education. As parents, we want to do everything we can to set our children up for success. Perhaps you have a child or a grandchild, and you're hoping to create an education fund that will be a conduit to a world of opportunities. Maybe you'd like to help them get a degree beyond high school without taking on any debt. Whether your child is still climbing the furniture, climbing the monkey bars, or climbing the high school ladder toward graduation, there are lots of ways you can invest in the future, including the benefits of a 529 plan.

Big Events. What is on your Bucket List? This could be a dream car you've always wanted to own, purchasing a diamond ring as you pop the question, planning for an anniversary destination, a home remodel, or anything else you choose. These are all things you need to save for, and retirement is not the only goal. You only get this one life, so it's a good idea to plan for it. As my wife and I work our way through our bucket list, we remind ourselves: **"We don't plan our adventures to escape life. We plan our adventures so that our lives don't escape us."**

Retirement goals. When do you want to retire? Most people stop working sometime between age fifty-five and seventy. While you may continue to receive income through Social Security, that monthly payment is not intended to be enough for most people to live comfortably. Most Americans aim to supplement their Social Security payments with additional retirement income. How much needs to be saved is different for everyone. It can vary from several hundred thousand to several million. Whatever the goal is, it will likely require decades of saving.

Independence. I meet with people whose financial goals have very little to do with luxurious lifestyles and high returns. They don't want to compete with the market – or with their colleagues. They simply want to wake up every day knowing that their family can make decisions on their terms, without borrowing from someone who has more money. All lifestyles exist on a spectrum, and what is a shortage to one person may feel like abundance to another. We don't all have to earn an extravagant salary to achieve independence. What matters are your goals, your lifestyle, and your plan.

Personalize Your Approach – and Be Honest with Yourself

When you plan for your financial future, clarify and align your goals from the very beginning. Just like traveling with someone whose goals are different from yours, you want to communicate your goals with your spouse and your advisor. If your advisor thinks you want to save for retirement in twenty years, but really, you want to take an anniversary trip in five years, the dreams will stay in the clouds – never in your hands. You don't have to be a genius to do it, but you do need to have a plan. You just need to know a few basics, form a plan, and be ready to stick to it so you can end up where you want to be. That's the path to living the life you have in mind.

If retirement is your priority, consider the benefits of tax-advantaged investments. Employer-sponsored retirement plans, such as 401(k)s, can be a great way to save because the money comes out of your paycheck before you even see it. Also, as an added incentive, some employers offer to match a percentage of your contributions.

For money you may want to access before retirement, place the funds in a separate account. When this hits your target, you may want to move the money into more growth-oriented investments that offer the potential for higher returns. Keep in mind, this may mean exposing your money to more volatility, so you'll want to choose vehicles that fit your risk tolerance, time horizon, and long-term goals.

Invest Now

Be honest with yourself. Honestly assess what you have, what you need, and what goals are realistic. After all, you will be the one to reap the benefits or the consequences of the risks of investing. If you are working with an advisor, make sure they know your goals.

So, How Much Should You Save?

There is no one-size-fits-all number or equation to answer this question, but I can offer you these general guidelines:

By the time you are thirty, save "your income x 1."

By the time you are forty, save "your income x 3."

By the time you are fifty, save "your income x 5."

By the time you are sixty, save "your income x 7."

By the time you are seventy, save "your income x 9."

To achieve these goals on this timeline, you generally need to save 15% of your gross income, and once again, starting early is the key to financial freedom. If you're in your twenties, it's not too early. If you're in your fifties, it's not too late. You may be starting a new career or paying back student loans, so do the best you can. Increase your level of savings when you receive raises. Down the road, you'll be thankful you made your financial goals one of your top priorities.

If your goal is to have $1 million when you retire, let's look at the value of starting early with the discipline of paying yourself first. Here's a graph showing how you might become a millionaire, based on a monthly savings, your age, and a 7%

return. If you start at age 16, you only need to invest $210 per month. If you start at age 50, you need to set aside a whopping $3300 per month.

Life happens! From retirement planning, saving for education, crossing off your bucket list items, or simply building a nest egg, individual investors may have a wide range of goals they hope to

achieve. A concrete investment plan can help keep you on track – and increase your chances of achieving your goals. Those who have money in savings are much better equipped to deal with these issues than those who have saved little or no money. Whatever your goals are, start toward them today.

Your decisions are not locked in stone, so you can make changes any time. I remind my clients to revisit their list of goals every three to five years, or after any major life change. When babies are born, grandparents die, and marriages begin or end, our goals shift and change. Don't beat yourself up if you don't meet your goals. Simply adjust your map and stay the course. The important thing is to get started today.

In the pursuit of growing wealth, sound habits can be your most valuable asset. Develop the habit of paying yourself first and get started today. The sooner you begin, the more potential your savings may have to grow.

CHAPTER THREE

The Quest to Invest
What is Investing?

"Compound interest is the eighth wonder of the world. He who understands it, earns it; he who doesn't, pays it."
~ Albert Einstein

A savings account is a great start, but what if there were a way to make that money grow more powerfully while you're doing other things—eating, driving, vacationing, working, and even sleeping? This is the attraction of investing. Your money grows and multiplies while you're busy living your life.

Investors are primarily driven by the chance to make their money grow. People invest to make more money, like planting a seed in the ground. With time and patience, those investments will grow through the magic of compounding or compound interest.

Investing is a long-term strategy of placing your money in a company, or several companies via pooled investment vehicles, that you believe to be successful and headed in a profitable direction.

When you invest, you can either be a lender or an owner.

If you choose to lend, you are letting someone else borrow your money to grow their business, and in return they agree to pay the money back to you–with interest.

When you purchase stock in a company, you choose to become an owner of that business. You own a percentage of their real estate, their earnings, their cash flow, their patents—their everything. You are participating in their growth. Your stock portfolio is not simply a collection of pieces of paper to be traded by the minute or the hour, but rather they are your ownership interests in those companies.

To borrow anything is to take and use something that belongs to someone else, with the intention of returning it. Lending is just the opposite: it is to grant to someone the use of something on the understanding that it shall be returned.

So, when you lend your money, it is the opposite of when you borrow money from someone. When you take out a $20,000 loan for a car, you know that you must pay back the principal plus interest. So, you may pay back $25,000 by the time the loan is

Principal: The amount of money the borrower owes the lender.

Interest: The fee the borrower pays to the lender, in exchange for the privilege of using the lender's money.

Financial Return: The amount of money the lender receives from an investment.

Dividend: The sum of money a company pays to its shareholders on a regular basis.

paid off. You are the borrower, and that is how the math works out for your end of the transaction.

But when you are the lender, you are receiving the interest instead of paying the interest. You are buying a bond in a company, and in return, the company promises to pay you interest on the money you lend to the company.

When you lend money as an investment, you are doing so to make a profit. Your principal (amount lent) accrues interest over the life of the bond, and ultimately your original investment comes back to you with interest earned on top. You are essentially the "Bank" in this situation.

Let's speak in the simplest of terms with the simplest of math. If you lend $100 at a 5% interest rate for one year, then at the end of that year you will get back $105. The original amount is called the principal and the profit is the interest earned.

When you purchase shares of a company, become an owner, you may also get paid back a portion of the profits called a **Dividend**. This is the payout of the stock, a returned portion of a company's earnings to the shareholder (owner) via a distribution of cash. Time has shown that the majority of the stock market return comes from the dividends. In fact, if we go back and look at the broad index of the S&P 500 over any ten-year period, nearly 70% of the total returns have come from dividends, versus growth in the price. Dividends are the workhorses of wealth accumulation, hard at work behind the scenes, providing consistent cash flow— especially if you reinvest those dividends back into the shares.

Invest Now

When you or I are paid a dividend from an investment, we may be tempted to spend that dividend and enjoy a nice steak dinner or a night on the town. But at the end of the night, that money is gone, and all we will have is a full belly that will be hungry again by morning. Instead of spending it on a frivolous activity, let's put that money right back into the market. Use that money to buy more stock, and watch our returns grow larger every year.

Simple interest will earn you a nominal amount, but the real power of investing is in Compound Interest. Buckle up – this is where the numbers really multiply!

Power of Compound Interest

Compound Interest[7] is calculated on that initial principal, *plus* the interest and earnings that accumulate every period. When you reinvest the interest or dividends, the gains in the next period are then earned on the principal sum, *plus* the previously accumulated payouts. You are making a rate of return *on your return*, earning gains on gains. When this process happens over and over, compounding grows your wealth at an exponential rate. This is what we are aiming for when we use the phrase, *making your money work for you.*[8]

Compounding interest is a snowball effect that grows a small amount of money into a larger amount over time. Investing is one of the most powerful things you can do to build wealth for the long-term, and compounding interest is the engine that makes it so powerful. This is the most powerful ingredient of successful investing. Many sources say Albert Einstein called it the eighth wonder of the world. Einstein said. **"He who understands it, earns it. He who doesn't, pays it**."[9] His words carry a tone of caution: if you're the

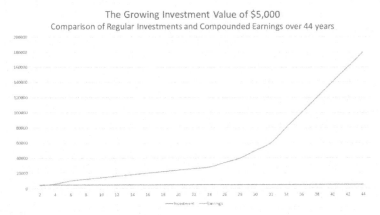

The Growing Investment Value of $5,000
Comparison of Regular Investments and Compounded Earnings over 44 years

one paying compound interest, then your money is working hard for someone else. For example, if you've ever tried to pay down a loan or credit card debt, but the balance never seems to go down, this is because of compound interest working against you. Your loan provider is adding to the burden of your debt as the amount you owe grows, requiring you to pay interest on interest.

If you're *paying* compound interest, your bills can add up to huge amounts over time. But if you're *earning* compound interest, your savings can add up to huge amounts over time. The choice is yours.

Investing is Different from Speculating

Invest Now

Companies are organic, not static. They grow and change, just like anything else that human beings do. Companies have management teams that move, adjust, and strategize to an ever-moving economy. Each company is led by a team of experts in their field, and they're utilizing their resources and collaborative ideas to steer the business in the right direction. While some

Investing

Expending money with the expectation of achieving a profitable result over a course of time and development.

Speculating

Trading money in the hope of quick gains, based on fleeting headlines and algorithms.

managements teams are certainly better than others, we can be sure that the team managing their company is almost always aware of "the dangers that lurk." Leaders make decisions like you make yours: with goals, coaching, and an eye on the long-term outcomes. The companies featured in today's headlines already know what's going on. They didn't wake up and discover on the morning news that things have taken a turn.

Remember how I told you about the loud headlines playing with our emotions, tempting us to make emotional decisions instead of rational choices? This is where that comes into play. Players on Wall Street often want us to think these business leaders are mindlessly riding the waves of the economy, paying no mind to business smarts, but that's not the case.

Every day, analysts on Wall Street change their recommendations on stocks, encouraging investors to buy, sell, or hold, based on a whim. They encourage speculation. Wall Street is suddenly alarmed or creating chatter about a company's demise. Suddenly yesterday's darling is today's nightmare—or vice versa. In most cases, you can be sure that the management team of that company is not surprised or caught off guard by the latest utterings of an analyst or the media. In reality, companies are moving along, day to day and quarter to quarter, efficiently allocating capital and creating long-term value.

(If they're not doing this, you don't want to invest in them in the first place.)

In today's instant gratification society, we seem to have obliterated the lines between investing and speculating – or gambling. In fact, most of the headlines today are far more about speculation than investing. What is the difference? How does investing compare to speculating?

Speculating is a short-term approach that involves taking high risks and expecting significant returns.

It's the difference between sailing across the ocean, versus riding the next wave that looks like it can carry you to shore. Investing is deep and slow, while speculation is shallow and fast, based on opinions and chatter that will dissolve by tomorrow.

When you invest, you are purchasing ownership in a company with the hope that it will create value over time, via dividends or an increased value of the company.

When you speculate, you are hoping to make some quick cash because of a trading chart, a complicated algorithm, or the most recent hype in the news.

A "Coca-Cola Classic" Example

Let's look at one famous difference between investing and speculating. When Warren Buffett's company first purchased stock in Coca-Cola in 1988, the company purchased more than 23 million shares—or one billion dollars—in the soft drink company. Wall Street analysts and media reporters believed this to be a risky venture, and Buffett's shareholders were concerned. What would become of the money invested in a company that made sugary drinks?

It wasn't an easy sell to his shareholders, and it hasn't been an easy haul for Coca-Cola. But their company is well managed by effective leaders who have managed the company through challenging times. For decades now, they have endlessly adjusted to market conditions, considering consumer preferences, diet fads, and health concerns. Yes, Coke sells sugary sodas, but they are also one of the largest sellers of bottled water, energy drinks, and teas.

Soon after Buffett's investment, the media raised questions and created hyper concerns, but Warren Buffett saw something deep and good in Coca-Cola, and his investors benefited from this wisdom. Buffett's company, Berkshire, never sold a share, and as of year-end 2020, the investment in Coca-Cola has grown to more than $21.5 billion, a return of 1550%, not including dividends.[10]

In his 1988 letter to Berkshire shareholders, Warren Buffett defended his investment decisions with a statement that has become one of the most famous aphorisms in the investing world: **"When we own a portion of outstanding businesses with outstanding managements, our favorite holding period is forever."**[11]

Investing is ownership in a business enterprise, not speculating on the short-term price swings of a piece of paper. Speculators are in and out, while investors are in for the long-term. Investors are the ones on a smooth plane to making money.

Investing in what you know means choosing companies with products familiar to you, and business models you understand. If you're wondering where to begin, look at the labels of the products you're buying, and then research the manufacturer. If you notice a chain of stores popping up all over your city, and you find you enjoy shopping there and have positive experiences, consider investing in that chain of stores. If there's a fast-food restaurant near you, and you've noticed that their drive-thru consistently has a line of cars stretched around the building, consider investing in that restaurant.

Ashton Kutcher said, "If you drink beer all the time—if you go to microbreweries and you try all kinds of them—you probably know which ones are the best, and my advice is always to invest in what you know."[12]

Don't ignore your own professional expertise. If you're a teacher, you know the success of book publishers in the academic world. If you're a software engineer, you have expertise in server set up and administration, so you might be best equipped to invest in a cloud computing sector. If you love to garden, perhaps you'd do well to invest in the agricultural sect.

But hear me on this: Do not skip the research. Your interest and investment in familiar products and services are not a substitute for the benefits of logic, smart choices, measuring performance, and researching the companies you're interested in. **Robert Kiyosaki clarified those famous words with his advice, "Don't invest in what you don't know. Learn first, then invest."** Investigate what they're doing that's making it work, and then invest in the companies you like, understand, and enjoy.

How can you know where to invest?
Invest in what you know.

CHAPTER FOUR

Build Your Foundation
Knowing the Tools

"Give us the tools, and we will finish the job."
~ Winston Churchill

If you and I were planning a trip, we might begin by googling our destination. Thanks to the wonders of the internet, that's a solid starting point. We would want to consider the local attractions, how to get around the city, and the best places to stay. We would want to find the best flights and the best times to travel, and we might even choose to learn some of the language. We could dig as deep as we choose into the culture we're planning to visit.

On the other hand, I also suspect we wouldn't need to know *all there is to know* about the place we plan to visit. We wouldn't need to get certified in the history of the city, and we wouldn't need to give a walking tour to our fellow tourists. That's a lot of information to process, and people can spend their whole lives diving deep into the many leagues of the sea of one topic.

Invest Now

What we probably would want, instead, is the experience of someone who has planned their own trip, visited our destinations, and can show us some nice pictures to heighten our understanding and anticipation. Now *that's* a good starting point.

Similarly, you do not need a degree in finance before you can understand your own investment journey. Yes, you could dive deep, get a dozen certificates, become an expert, and start your own business. But you likely want someone else to navigate the graphs and numbers, and you'd like a basic understanding

Savings:
A bank account that earns interest. You can withdraw your money at any time.

CD:
A certificate of deposit. Like a savings account, money earns interest, but you cannot withdraw your money until a set date.

Bond:
A loan of cash toward a business or government that uses your money to fund their needs, paying you interest in return. Generally, a bond earns more interest than a savings or CD.

and some pictures to show you how your money can grow. There are a handful of terms, tools, and concepts that all investors should understand, and you've come to the right place to get started. When you have built a foundation, you can move onto more complicated layers of the process.

First Options

How can you get started earning interest? We can earn a small amount of interest by putting your money into a **savings account** or a **CD, Certificate of Deposit.** Available at banks and credit unions, these accounts are very similar with one major difference: a customer with a regular savings account can withdraw their money at any time, while customers who purchase CDs must leave their money in the account for a specified length of time. CDs usually offer a slightly higher rate of interest, since the bank knows exactly how long they will have use of the money. (If you withdraw from the CD before the agreed time, you'll have to pay a hefty penalty. So, it's best to let that money sit, untouched.)

Savings accounts and CDs do not offer a high financial return, but they are low risk because they almost always return a guaranteed rate of interest over time. If you're looking to earn more than the limited interest payments of a savings account or CD, then your next consideration might be a bond.

Net Asset Value (NAV):

The price of a share or bond at a specific date or time. The NAV shifts based on the company's total assets, minus its liabilities.

A **bond** is essentially a loan to a government or business who needs to raise money quickly and easily. The money is often utilized to fund various projects, such as repairing roads and bridges, building projects, and expansion plans.

When you purchase a bond, you do not own any part of the business, but you are lending money toward their success. A bond generally yields a specific interest rate, so a bond that yields 2% will return to you the principal, plus 2% annually.

It's important to remember that bond prices rise and fall on a daily basis. The principal value will fluctuate, and the bond may lose principal during a period of rising interests. But if a bond is held to maturity, then you will receive the original principal and interest promised.

Still, these accounts, certificates, and bonds appeal to savers because they have a guaranteed rate of return. CDs are insured by the Federal Deposit Insurance Corp (FDIC) up to $250,000. If you deposit money into one of these accounts, and if you leave your money there for a reasonable stretch of time, the money will grow—though not by much. People who are looking for higher potential rewards often choose to invest their money in a **share of a company**, also called a **stock**. Essentially, the largest American companies are owned not by individuals, but by many different people. Ownership is divided into pieces, called stocks or shares. Each piece can be publicly traded, which means it can be bought or sold on an exchange.

Publicly traded companies are listed on various stock exchanges, labeled and recognized by their own **stock symbol.** If you invest in a share or stock—congratulations! —you are a shareholder, and you own a piece of the business. As part owner, you do not get to make decisions for the corporation, but if the business does well, you will receive a percentage of their profits, and hopefully the share price will grow over time.

When you purchase individual stocks, for the most part you are in control of the taxation of your investments. If you don't sell, you don't pay capital gain taxes. If you choose to have dividends or not will determine income taxes. These things are within your control.

What are Mutual Funds and Exchange Traded Funds?

Mutual funds and Exchange Traded Funds (ETFs) allow investors to pool their money in portfolios of stocks, bonds, and other securities. These are low-cost tools to diversify your investments and receive professional management services that typically would not be available to smaller investors.

While similar in nature, mutual funds and ETFs are actually very different. ETF's allow people to have professional management at a relatively low cost, and they allow you to instantly diversify your investments and take away some of the more complicated decisions of investing in individual stocks. However, you also give up some control when

Share or Stock:
A small piece of ownership of a large company. A shareholder is an investor who owns shares of stock. They are part owner of the company, and they earn a percentage of the company's profits.

Stock Symbol
The letters used to identify listed companies on the exchanges where they are traded.

investing in Mutual Funds and ETFs, as your particular circumstances are not a part of the manager decision making process There can be thousands—or tens of thousands—of people who have invested in the same mutual fund or ETF along with you.

When you purchase or sell a mutual fund, you are transacting at the fund's value at the end of the trading day, a fixed price known as the **NAV, or Net Asset Value.** An ETF can be traded throughout the day, like a stock, and its price may fluctuate by the minute. These price differences can carry important weight, and they often have consequences.

Income-oriented mutual funds focus on generating current income, either on a monthly or quarterly basis. Shares are constantly sold or purchased, and the cost of each share fluctuates on a daily basis. When you purchase a share when the cost is low, and you sell when the cost is high, you get to profit the difference—which can be an impressive amount. For example, a stock that is purchased at $10 and goes up to $15 has 50% return. This is a much faster profit than any savings account or CD.

Other differences include the size of the fees, taxes, and distributions. Generally speaking, but not always true, mutual funds tend to have a higher management fee than ETF's. According to a

Morningstar

A financial service firm providing investment research and management services. Morningstar's research and recommendations are highly influential in the industry of asset management.

recent study by Morningstar, the **average ETF expense ratio was 0.23%**, compared with the average expense ratio of 0.73% for index mutual funds and 1.45% for actively managed mutual funds.

While there are exceptions to every rule, ETFs are generally more tax efficient than Mutual funds. As a result, ETF's can grow without taxable distributions for long periods of time, meaning they are often tax free until sold.

A mutual fund generally pays out distributions annually, and these are taxable events. This is irrelevant if the funds are held in an IRA or other tax deferred account, but they can have important consequences if held in a taxable brokerage account.

Active Portfolio Management
Focuses on outperforming the market in comparison to specific benchmarks, such as the S&P 500.
Passive Portfolio Management
Mimics the investment holdings of a particular index, in order to achieve similar results.

Which is Best?

Well, investing is complicated, and there is never a guarantee that you will make money from your investments. It is a personal choice for you to make. In the end, there is not right or wrong way to go, and you can always do both. It really comes down to your comfort level, as well as how much time you want to put into your investment decisions.

In each case—savings, CDs, bonds, stocks, and mutual funds—you are investing money, and you are seeking a return on your investment. It's important to understand a portfolio's overall return, and it's far more important to develop a sound investment strategy than it is to pick individual stocks. When you have a sound investment strategy, you plant an acorn that grows into an oak tree.

CHAPTER FIVE

Navigating those Highs and Lows
Meet the Bull and the Bear

"He who lives by the crystal ball soon learns to eat ground glass." ~ Edgar R. Fiedler, 1929–2003
(Assistant Secretary of the Treasury during the presidencies of Richard Nixon and Gerald Ford)

Next, let's see what you need to know about navigating the highs and lows of the market.

Points and Percentages

As you navigate the market, you will hear terms used interchangeably: points and percentages. You might hear "The market dropped by one thousand points," or "The market went up by two percent." A point is the equivalent of one dollar. As I write this, the DOW is at approximately 35,000 points. That number changes every day.

When they say that the market dropped by 1,000 points, that's less than 3%. News commentators usually talk about points because it sounds more sensational—and often scarier—to say, "The DOW is down by a thousand points." They are literally trying to get us to panic. (Perhaps I've mentioned this before: turn off the noise.)

Dow Jones, S&P 500, and NASDAQ

You've likely heard these terms tossed around: Dow Jones, the S&P 500 and NASDAQ. Who and what are these? Each one is a stock market index, or a tool that measures stock performance by collecting financial data from different companies and industries. Some indexes track a handful of stocks, and others track thousands at a time.

Let's start with **Dow Jones**.[13] It sounds like the name of a person, right? It

---

"The Dow"

A number representing the average price of 30 of the largest and most widely traded stocks in the United States.

S&P 500

A number tracking the performance of 500 of the largest stocks in the United States. The S&P 500 is generally considered the best indicator of how U.S. stocks are performing overall.

NASDAQ

An index that includes nearly 5,000 companies, predominately focused on technology.

---

actually began as a company founded by three guys in the late 1800s. Dow was an early financial guru, and he became famous for his ability to predict movement in the stock market—and to explain financial news to the public. He discovered that it was possible to predict movements across the market by watching the rise and decline of a certain list of stocks. The Dow Jones Company compiled an index of thirty stocks, ultimately the best stocks in their industry. This is called the Dow Jones Industrial 30, and you'll often hear it called "the Dow."

The original companies operated in railroads, cotton, gas, sugar, tobacco, and oil[14]—the leading industries whose collective health could reflect the overall health of the economy. Today, the Dow Jones Industrial Average (DJIA) has become one of the most watched stock indexes in the world. The index continues to be a list of thirty companies that represent the best stocks in their industry, now including names like Apple, Boeing, Microsoft, and Coca-Cola—companies we all recognize.

The Dow is measured in points, and essentially a point is equivalent to $1 US dollar in stock prices. When the Dow Jones began in May 1896, the industrial average was 40.94 points, and that number has increased significantly in the last two centuries. In 2022 it surpassed 36,000 points.[15] If you hear that the Dow went up 25 points, this means it would cost approximately $25 USD more to buy the same stocks today than it would have cost on the previous business day.[16]

The **S&P 500** is a broader index which tracks 500 of the largest stocks in the market. This index was introduced in 1957, and it is maintained by the Standard & Poor's Index Committee. This index gives us a greater depth and breadth of what is going on in the public market throughout the trading day, because it represents the number of shares available for public trading, including technology firms and financial businesses.[17] The list of companies changes often, as there are several criteria that companies must meet to be included in the S&P 500.

Contrary to popular belief, the S&P 500 is not a collection of the largest companies in America, but rather a collection large-cap stocks from a broad range of market sectors, including technology, health care, and consumer staples, among others. The S&P 500 updates appear everywhere—on the news, in the papers, and they are often a measurement tool for comparing our own investments' performance. This index contains the companies most widely owned by individual investors, so **the S&P 500** is generally considered the best indicator of how U.S. stocks are performing overall.[18]

The **NASDAQ** is a third index, which includes nearly 5,000 stocks, including tech, biotech, and more aggressive stocks.

These three markets go up and down every day. On the evening news and even at family gatherings, you'll often hear people talk about whether the market is up, down, or how it is performing. They are asking about an overall direction of stock prices, as reflected by the price movement of the Dow, the S&P, and the NASDAQ.

Stock Market Corrections

The stock market is generally growing, but as we have discussed, there are also occasional dips, called **Market Corrections.** A stock market correction is usually defined as a drop in stock prices of 10% or more from their recent peak. They occur about every 8 to 12 months, and on average, they last about 54 days.[19]

Corrections can be nerve-wracking as you watch your portfolio dip, but corrections are also a sign of a healthy market in most cases. Don't panic and trade on market corrections. Remember that it is often best to just ride them out.

Generally speaking, the market is not a reflection at today's conditions, but actually a forecast of a year from now. Today's headlines reflect what will move the market in the next 12-18 months. Sometimes national or global emergencies happen – like when the Twin Towers fell on September 11, when a President has been assassinated, or the sudden onset of the Coronavirus – and these crises can cause a

Large-Cap Stocks

Stock in larger companies that have a market capitalization of over $10 billion.

Small-Cap Stocks

Stock in smaller companies that have a market capitalization between $300 million to $2 billion.

Market Capitalization

The market's current estimate of the total dollar value of a company's outstanding stock.

huge, short term drops in the market. But mostly, the ups and downs of the market reflect what investors expect in the future.

The Bull and The Bear

When the market goes up, we have what is called a **Bull Market.** This is a stretch of time, at least two months, with rising stock prices of more than 20%. This tends to reflect a strong economy that is getting stronger still, and it's a time when investors have high confidence and optimism. A bull market is a rising market, and investors are making money and looking to buy more.

When the market goes down, we have what is called a **Bear Market.** This is a stretch of time, at least two months, when market prices have declined twenty percent or more from their highs. We also expect to see drops of 5-10% every year, and those are just corrections. Share prices are dropping, investors are discouraged, and there is a general sense of pessimism about the future. A bear market has a downward slope, and many investors sell their holdings, looking to get out of the market.

> *Market Corrections*
> *A drop of 10% or more from the most recent highs in the Dow, S&P 500, or Nasdaq.*

Even When the Headlines are Right

While the market's long-term trend is always up, there are bumps along the way, and some are larger than others. Sometimes the headlines are right, and sometimes the market does go down.

You've seen this, and I have, too.

The very worst crash in stock market history happened in 1929, when the Roaring Twenties sank into the Great Depression. In the eight years prior to the crash, from 1921 to September1929, the market had soared exponentially, rising nearly six-fold. The Twenties were a time of prosperity, and the economy soared higher and higher. But in September 1929, some cracks started to show in the market. There was a two-day climax in October—now known as Black Monday and Black Tuesday—but by Friday, the market was 25% lower than it had been at the start of the week. The market had begun to plummet, and by mid-November 1929, the market had lost 50% of its value. The downward spiral continued into the summer of 1932, landing at a gut-wrenching low of 89% below its peak a few years earlier. The Great Depression expanded into a worldwide problem, the longest, deepest, and most widespread depression of the 20th century. Twenty years passed before the market regained its pre-crash high.

That crash happened long before you and I were born, and in fact I wrote a thesis paper on The Great Depression when I was in college. It was long-ago history, sure to never repeat itself . . . or so I thought.

I remember it well: the Black Monday Crash of 1987. I was a young intern, new to the industry, when the market plunged nearly 22% on October 19, 1987. It was the worst single-day decline in market history, even to this day. Every indication pointed to another Great Depression that would knock us down all over again. But this was different from the plunge sixty years prior: this decline was caused more by program trading than economic failure, and the market began to recover just a few weeks later, in November of 1987. In less than two years, the market had recouped all its losses.

More than twenty years ago, there was a lot of concern about the phenomenon of Y2K, a buzzing fear that computers would stop working on December 31, 1999. There were intense preparations, programming corrections, and so many phone calls to financial advisors as people feared that this computer bug would be the end of the world. People were worried, and they wanted to sell all of their investments to protect their nest eggs.

Do you recall what happened on the morning of January 1, 2000? Very few failures. Yes, there were a few problems in the United States and around the world, but nothing to match the hype. The problems did not match the level of panic. The people who got out of the market were sorry that they did. The people who stayed invested, keeping their eye on the long-term goals, did just fine.

A few years later, we experienced the financial crisis of 2008, created by loose credit and bad lending practices, which were encouraged and even codified by Congress. Between October 2007 and March 2009, the market fell 54%, sometimes in large daily sell offs. It took four years for the Dow to recover, while other indices recovered even quicker. The market didn't need ages to recover, because the economy was taking off again.

There's a democratic occurrence that happens every four years that tends to wreak havoc on the emotions of people: presidential elections. When President Obama was elected, all the conservative investors and talking heads were saying, "It's the end of the world. Sell everything." But they were wrong. The market kept going up. When President Trump was elected, all the liberal investors and talking heads were saying, "It's the end of the world. Sell everything."

But they were wrong. The market went up—massively.

The most recent crash should still be fresh in our minds: Coronavirus 2020. However, that recovery happened so quickly that most of us have already forgotten that the crash happened at all. On March 12, the market fell nearly 10% due to the media's panic porn surrounding the pandemic. It was the largest single-day drop since 1987, and another plunge came just four days later—dropping another 12.9%. Even still, the market recovered, and this time, it recovered in weeks instead of months or years.

The Ebb and Flow of the Economic Cycle

Like seasons, months, weeks, days, and nights, the economy operates on a cycle that repeats. Though the pattern is called a cycle, it is often unpredictable, and usually not regular and or even cyclical. The business cycle moves like waves, rising and falling. We do not know when the cycles will shift, but we can predict this general movement: the economy will grow for a long time, then enter perhaps a steep recession, and then make a correction and continue back up in growth.

Recoveries occur when the economic situations improve over time, and recessions occur when those same indicators go down over time. Both recoveries and recessions can each last for as long as several years, or as little as a few months. A recession that is long or severe is called a depression.

How can we predict which stocks will grow, and when? Well, consider your own spending habits, related to the state of your budget. If you're like most people, your emotions and enthusiasm probably rise and fall with your financial accounts. When there is extra money in the "bank," you might feel happy, excited, hopeful for the future. You might decide now is the time to finish the basement, upgrade the family vehicle, put new carpet in the house, or take a vacation. When times are good, you feel confident to spend on luxury goods.

When money is tight, you might feel concerned about making money last. You probably tend to tighten up the budget, cut out extra spending, and pay attention to the differences between wants and needs. You might want to put new carpets in the house, but you may choose instead to move the furniture to cover the red wine stain. You may wish to go on a vacation, but you opt for a staycation instead, staying at home and watching movies that take place in Europe. You may wish for a new iPhone, but you decide to wait and see if this model can last another year. When money is tight, we are careful where we spend our money, and we save it for necessities.

Since these patterns are true for us as individuals, consider how the effect plays out across the economy, creating these economic cycles.

During a rebound or an upswing, we tend to be a little more jovial with our spending, so the stocks that deliver the highest returns are those invested in the "extras" of life: travel, real estate, discretionary spending. Your stocks will perform well if you have invested in industries producing innovative technology, construction materials, and items related to the travel industry (car rentals, luggage, airplanes, etc.).

During a recession or a recovery, we tend to pump the brakes and spend money only where we must, so the stocks that deliver the highest returns are those invested in the "necessities" of life: health care, utilities, energy, and consumer staples. Your stocks will do well if you have invested in industries producing toilet paper, electricity, and prescription drugs.

Why is this important to know? As our spending patterns shift, stocks take turns delivering returns throughout the economic cycle. They don't always grow at the same time. Investors who understand that the economic cycle moves through these periods of rise and fall will have a better perspective and understanding of where we are in the patterns of growth and recession. These investors will recognize when their current investments are likely to deliver returns, and when it may be time to re-allocate their funds differently for better performance.

Buying the Dip

To "Buy the Dip" is to purchase an asset after it has dropped in price. It's like buying something on sale, to sell it later at full price. The idea is that the new lower price is a bargain, and the price is likely to bounce back with time.

In January of 2022 we saw one of the most volatile days in market history. The market, as measured by the Dow Jones Industrial Average (DJIA) started the day at its lowest point, down 1,000+ points. However, by end of the day, the market had recouped its losses, and it closed the day up 100 points. Let's consider what this means.

Remember: Success is found not in timing the market, but with time in the market.

If you had decided to try and take advantage of the "dip" in the market that day, and if you had put $1,000 to work in a mutual fund when the market was down, your purchase would not have actually gone through until the end of the day. You would have transacted at a value NAV that would have reflected the day's end value of the market, which was up 100 points. You would have missed your opportunity to buy on the dip.

On the other hand, if you bought an equity ETF at the exact moment, it would have transacted in the moment you put your order in. You would have purchased when the market was actually down 1,000 points, and you likely would have closed out the day with a gain.

Of course, the opposite is also true. The market could be up at the time of purchase, and then down by the end of the day. While these extreme situations are rare and have little consequence on the return of your investments over time, it is important to understand the differences between the two.

There is a myth that success is based on *timing the market*, and there are maxims in investing that say things like, "Buy Low, Sell High." Yes, ideally, we would all like to buy stocks when the market is at the bottom and sell them when the market is at its peak. If only it were that easy, if those highs and lows showed up like holidays on a calendar. Unfortunately, that's just not how it works.

We've talked about this before, but it's worth repeating in this chapter. Investors who find success have learned the opposite is true: success is found not with timing the market, but with *time in the market*.

"This Time It's Different"

"This time is different." These may be the costliest words in investing.

In the early days of the pandemic, I received a call from a client who said, "Sean, we need to sell everything. This is really bad."

I gently tried to calm him down. Yes, it was bad, but to sell everything would be a huge mistake. Certain assets classes and stocks will do well during the pandemic, while others will likely go through a correction.

My client said, "How can you possibly know that? You've never been through a global pandemic. Nobody has."

Fair enough. I hadn't been through a pandemic. However, I've been through plenty of market shocks, from 9/11, y2k, bank failures, presidential assassination attempts, and many other headline events that rocked the world. And they always work out pretty much the same. In the end, it's about companies and earnings, not the latest panic porn being hyped by the media.

During the pandemic certain industries soared while others suffered. Many cloud-based internet companies grew so fast they had met their 5-year goals in just a few months. They were skyrocketing in price. On the other hand, energy stocks were plummeting at the prospect of a long and deep pandemic-led economic downturn.

There is no single type of investment that will always be the best one. There is a time for bonds, a time for blue chip stocks, and a time for small cap stocks. There is a time for international equities, and a time to focus on domestic equities. All of these trends are best met not by emotion, but by process. Our long-term success grows when we have a plan in place to weather the storm – the plan that is right for you. No strategy is perfect, but with these principles in mind, we are likely to have a positive long-term experience with investing.

Essentially, when we understand the economic cycle, we are less prone to panic during the rough times in the market. There are still good investment decisions to be made in both the highs and lows of the market, as well as in different areas of investing. This is the benefit of a diversified approach, of not "putting all your eggs in one basket."

In the next chapter, we will talk about how to diversify: how to spread your eggs into different baskets, and even to vary within those baskets with different shapes and sizes.

CHAPTER SIX

Don't Put All Your Eggs in One Basket
Diversifying Your Portfolio

"Asset allocation, where to park your money and how to divide it up, is the single most important skill of a successful investor." ~ Tony Robbins,
(Money: Master the Game: 7 Simple Steps to Financial Freedom)

Let's imagine an investor who has $600,000 to invest. There are many ways an investor could choose to invest this money, with varying degrees of risk and reward.

They could put all of their money in one stock and hope for the best. This investment plan has no diversity, and if the market dips – or even if the company has a difficult quarter – the investor could be subject to heavy losses. It's a high-risk proposition to put all your

money in one place. Consider the middle option. This is the first level of diversifying, when the investor puts that same amount into three different asset classes: stocks, bonds, and cash. These three classes are usually not correlated, so investors do not stand to lose as much if one of the other areas hit a rough patch. If one asset performs poorly, the other two may offset the loss, or at least soften what could have been a dramatic drop in the portfolio.

Level One Diversified

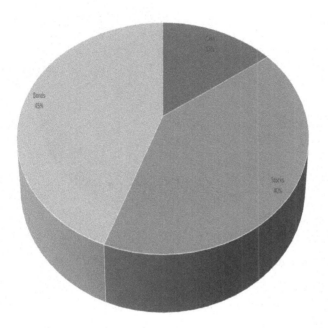

Still a third option remains, this is an example of that same amount divided into three classes, and then further diversified within those classes. They may choose to invest in stocks, bonds, and cash – and within those categories, they choose varying companies, and different bonds. Diversification suggests that your portfolio will yield a higher return and could pose less volatility than any individual investment.

Level Two Diversified

Asset Allocation

There is more to diversification than just spreading your money around. The goal is to diversify in investments that do not correlate with one another, so their gains and losses do not occur at the same as the other investments. If you have all your investments allocated to one category, you stand to lose a lot of money if that class takes a hit. This is where **asset allocation** becomes an important factor and a useful tool to manage systematic risk.[20]

Stocks and cash alternatives have different levels of risk and return, and asset allocation is the process of dividing investment dollars among various classes. As you diversify, you aim to manage your risk by spreading out your investments. This process helps guard against investment loss but also provides a smoother ride.

Shifts in the stock market can be brutal for investors. When some share prices fall with no end in sight, this is when asset allocation plays its key role. No stocks are immune to events of the market, but different stocks are affected differently, and some stock market sectors hold up better than others.

For example, especially during the pandemic, the economy stalled, and so did the demand for energy commodities like oil and gas. Commodity prices and stocks started to tumble. At the same time, technology boomed, as people worked from home, exploring the merits of virtual meetings and cloud technologies. Tech stocks soared, while energy stocks plummeted.

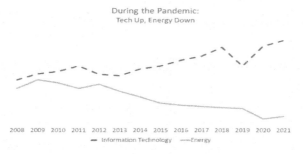

During the Pandemic: Tech Up, Energy Down

2008 2009 2010 2011 2012 2013 2014 2015 2016 2017 2018 2019 2020 2021
— Information Technology ——Energy

Asset allocation can lower the volatility of your portfolio, as you invest in equities with low **correlation**.[21] Ideally, it evens out the playing field, so that riskier assets are offset by those less risky. If one investment takes a dip, the fall isn't quite so far. Investors need to find the right mix that aligns with their risk tolerance and their investment timeline, by choosing assets from various classes. When you diversify your portfolio, you want to choose investments that belong to various asset classes with low correlation.

Asset Classes

When you were in elementary school, you probably learned the skill of classification, those simple exercises for grouping items and facts according to what they have in common. In science class, you might have classified animals according to their color, number of legs, type of skeleton, or internal features. Like many aspects of our adult lives, this concept is built on something we learned so long ago, that we may not even remember a time when we didn't understand it—and it applies here.

An **asset class** is a group of comparable investments, according to how they behave in the market, how they are taxed, and their same laws and regulations.[22]

Successful diversification is two levels deep, and effective

Asset Allocation

An investment strategy of dividing your investment dollars among various classes, to offset the risks involved.

Correlation

A measurement tool to show how two securities move in relation to one another. Do they grow together? Drop together? Or not affect one another?

investors diversify both between and within different asset classes. They vary their investments among stocks, bonds, cash, and alternatives—and within those classes, they have varying stocks, bonds, and cash alternatives. Since stocks do not all grow at the same time, a wise investor will diversify their investments across a portfolio of options that do not affect one another. That way when one falls, another can hopefully rise, and vice versa.

Why Diversify?

Imagine a stock portfolio that included a computer company, a software developer, and an internet service provider. Although the portfolio has spread its risk among three companies, all of them are related to one another: they all belong to the technology industry. People get very excited about the money-making opportunities inherent in new technology, but the risk is high.

The dot com bubble is a perfect example of why you can't put all your eggs in one basket, or even in one type of investment. The Nasdaq is a tech heavy index, and when internet technology became all the rage in the early 2000's, stock prices skyrocketed. Investors were eager to invest, and some of them put all their money in tech stocks—that would fall nearly 77% from March 2001 to October 2002. This area of the market required almost 15 years to regain its March 2001 high. As a financial advisor, this became a shining example of diversification.

Some financial research has shown that 91.5% of investment performance is determined by the asset allocation.[23] It can be difficult to know where to begin to invest, and these classes of assets can give you some direction on where to begin, depending on how much money you have to invest and how long you can let it grow.

There are three primary investment asset classes: **Equities** (stocks), **Fixed Income** (bonds), and **Cash Equivalents** (money market instruments). These days, most investment professionals also include real estate, commodities, and even cryptocurrencies in the asset class mix.

Generally, these types of investments are not correlated to one another, so they do not necessarily rise and fall together. If the market is down 50%, these assets are likely down or even up, depending on the economic conditions. This is the goal of diversification.

Let's look at some of these vehicles that allow you to diversify and invest safely for the long run.

Mutual Funds and **ETF (Exchange Traded Funds)** are popular among investors, as the money goes into an accumulated pool that is invested toward one goal or objective. They may have

Equities: Stocks or shares in a company. When you buy stocks, you're buying equities.

Mutual Fund or ETF: An accumulated pool of money, invested toward a common goal.

REIT: (Real Estate Investment Trust) An investment in real estate properties.

MLP: (Master Limited Partnership) A company organized by a combination of partners: General partners, who manage the company and oversee its operations, and limited partners, who are investors in the company.

a narrow objective, like the auto sector, or they may have a broader objective with a number of larger, well-known stocks.

A **Real Estate Investment Trust (REIT)** is an investment in real estate properties, in which the investor makes most of their money from rental or lease income. These usually include office buildings, retail spaces, apartments, assisted-living facilities, medical facilities, along with hotels or vacation resorts. REITs trade like stocks, and they tend to have big dividends, making it possible for everyday Americans to benefit from real estate. The stockholders of a REIT earn a share of the income produced from the real estate, without having to physically buy, manage, maintain, and finance property.[24]

A **Master Limited Partnership** (MLP)[25] is a company organized as a publicly traded partnership, so it combines two types of partners: general partners who own the business and oversee its operations, and limited partners, who invest in the company. MLPs are popular because have large dividends, they offer tax advantages, and they return the majority of their cash to unitholders. As partnerships, MLPs do not pay state or federal corporate income tax. Instead, their tax liability is passed on to their investors, who are then taxed on these distributions at their income tax rate. This isn't a permanent escape from taxation, but rather a deferral of taxation until a later date—usually the time when you sell the partnership interest. Investors can benefit by investing in MLPs because they are less correlated with other asset classes.

Invest Now

Cryptocurrencies[26] are a virtual currency, meaning they are only available in digital or electronic form. You cannot hold cryptocurrency in your hand, just like you cannot hold the internet in your hand. It exists only in electronic form, and all transactions are stored in software and computer applications. This financial structure does not happen in banks or institutions, so it exists outside the control of governments and central authorities—but the IRS still wants a piece of the profits if you reap some capital gains by selling or trading your cryptocurrency. Investors benefit from virtual currencies because they are fast and easy, but there are disadvantages to utilizing such new technology. Software is vulnerable to hackers, and there is not yet much legal recourse to investors because these methods are new and not yet regulated. In fact, I just heard from a client who had ten thousand dollars in cryptocurrency stolen from them, by a hacker.

Taxable Assets

Anytime anyone makes any money, the government wants a piece of it. You'll always have to pay a tax—that much is guaranteed. However, some assets require you to begin to pay taxes when you purchase the equity or begin to earn the income stream, and others defer the taxes until you sell the position. You won't get out of paying them, but you won't have to pay them all right away. This is part of asset allocation, and we will talk more about taxable assets as we talk about planning your retirement.

Financial Buckets: Your Income Sources

If we plan carefully, your retirement income will stream through several different "buckets" that we've created all along the way. Now is the time to decide how you are going to pay for the retirement you're hoping to enjoy. Of course, we all know that life doesn't come with guarantees, but a solid and sound investment strategy is a great foundation to equip you to pursue your retirement dreams. These could include 401(k), IRAs, CDs or rental real estate income, annuities, brokerage accounts, a pension or Social Security, and personal savings. All of these buckets may create income, and each bucket plays a different role in your retirement.

Take stock. Retirement planning is simply a map to ensure you have financial resources available when you're no longer generating income from your labor. Essentially, as we've said – you've spent a lifetime working for your money, now it's time to make your money work for you. Your plan depends on some important factors, and the makeup of each person's portfolio may be entirely different, depending on the emotionality of the individual, the risks they are willing to take, and the timing of their retirement.

401(k) Bucket

The 401(k) is a natural, attainable way to begin your savings and retirement plan. It is such a common approach that the words

"401(k)" have become nearly synonymous with retirement, as it is usually a retiree's largest bucket – or one of the largest.

The 401(k) is low maintenance, but everything is handled by someone else. This retirement savings plan is a *defined contribution plan* sponsored by your employer. Employees who participate in a traditional 401(k) plan have a portion of their pre-tax salary withdrawn from their paycheck, invested directly in the option(s) they choose, and often the employer will match a percentage of the employee's contribution. If your employer offers a match of any kind, then you have a good 401(k).

What makes the 401(k) so powerful? These words: **tax deferred contribution**.

Imagine you earn $100,000, and you have chosen to contribute $10,000 to your 401(k). That $10,000 will be deducted from your paycheck, and you would not pay the taxes that would ordinarily have been due the year the money was earned. The taxman will eventually come to get his cut, but you won't pay those taxes until much later on, when you withdraw the funds for your retirement. Since you won't be in the workforce and earning a regular paycheck during that retirement, you'll be in a lower tax bracket, which means your tax rate will be lower.

IRA – Individual Retirement Account

Just about anyone can open an IRA, Independent Retirement Account, and if you're a hardcore planner, then the IRA could be your ideal option. If you're willing to put in a bit more time to learn the language of the IRA savings, you can build a strong nest egg for your future.

IRAs are tax-advantaged investments, and there are two types: Roth IRA and traditional IRA. They are identical if the tax rate is the same now or later, when you contribute or withdraw. For most people, their tax rate shifts throughout their lifetime, based on their age and income. So, for most people, the timing of the tax makes a significant difference.

When you contribute to a **Traditional IRA**, you make contributions without taking taxes out yet. When you withdraw the funds in many years, you pay taxes then.

When you contribute to a **Roth IRA,** you can pay taxes the year you make the contribution, instead of the year you take the money out. There's no immediate tax break – but when you take money out in years to come, you won't pay taxes.

Younger savers are wise to put their money into a Roth 401(k) or Roth IRA, long before they reach their peak earnings and higher tax brackets. Also, if you anticipate that your tax rate may be higher when you retire, then a Roth IRA may be a better plan for you.

A Few Words about Life Insurance

First, the best life insurance is the least expensive policy. Put as little money into it as possible. If you can get a term life insurance policy that pays you a million dollars for $50 a month,

Life Insurance:
Buy term.
Invest the rest.

do that. What you *don't* need in most cases is the policy that costs 20k a year and builds up cash value. If you have $20k to put aside each year, invest that money into the market—not into a life insurance plan. Put $50 toward your life insurance policy and put the rest into the market. Here's a maxim you can trust: Buy Term, Invest the Rest.

Second, don't view life insurance as an investment. Life insurance is not an investment you can enjoy, because you have to die to get it.

Consider this example: You don't pay insurance on your house and view it as an investment. The reality is, you hope you'll never have to cash in that insurance, because that will mean you have lost your home. You only get the money if your house is destroyed. It's a catastrophic situation that you don't want.

In the same way, life insurance is a gift to the people you leave behind. But it is not money you will personally ever enjoy, because that check won't be cashed until you're gone.

Keep your life insurance and your investments separate. They are two very different things.

Rebalancing Your Portfolio

Asset allocation is not a "One-and-Done" task. It is an ongoing assessment of market performance, but it is also an organic process that evolves along with your major life events. From time to time, you'll need to rebalance your portfolio to meet your goals and achieve the stability of growth and return that you want. The average investor will do a rebalance once a year. Over time, a portfolio may look very different from when you began investing.

There are two ways to rebalance: the first is to sell some of your investments to raise sufficient cash to purchase a different investment. The other way is to use money that you're adding to your portfolio to adjust the asset classes to the level you desire. Whenever new cash is available, it is most effective to use that money to rebalance your portfolio.

Let's say you have allocated your assets so that you invest 10% in asset class A, and 15% in asset class B. At the end of the year, A has dipped down to 8%, while B has grown to 17%. You could rebalance your portfolio by selling two percent of your assets in Class B, and reinvesting them by buying more stock in Class A.

Ideally, this rebalance evens out the ride a little bit, keeping your assets approximately aligned with your retirement goals.

Remain Flexible and Diversified

Flexibility and diversification are often the keys to successful investing. Nobody ever knows what is next for the short-term of the

Rebalancing Your Portfolio

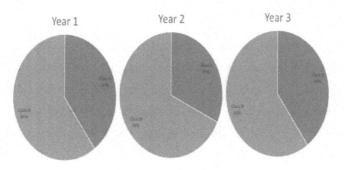

market, and your best strategy is to remain adaptable and varied with your assets.

For example, consider the energy sector of the market. This is the collective of companies and industries that involve the production and sale of energy, including oil, gas, and fuel. Over the last three years, the energy sector was up only 10.6% —by far the worst among the 11 sectors of the S&P 500. But as I write this paragraph, Russia has just invaded Ukraine. As a result, oil prices are through the roof, and energy is the only positive sector in the stock market year to date. It's up a whopping 27 percent, while most of the market is suffering a 10+ percent correction.[27]

Since we cannot predict these events, a portfolio that is well diversified can often be the great equalizer, filling your buckets that began to run low. If you allocated some of their assets to energy in 2021, back when it was one of the market's worst performing sectors, then there's a payoff now: those same assets are greatly outperforming the rest of the market in 2021.

The short-term moves of the market tend to be driven by events that affect the whole world. A pandemic, natural disasters, war, or other unforeseen events can quickly change the short-term trajectory of the market. For ten years now, most investors have been expecting interest rates to increase and bonds to get hammered. "This is the year," they tell us. While this forecast makes sense, it hasn't happened because other events keep causing a rush to safety. When unexpected and scary events occur, the rush to safety is often the answer of the institutional investors.

Even still, we cannot let ourselves get caught up in the headlines, letting them make all our decisions. Today's flashiest headline is likely to be nothing more than a distant memory a year from now. When your portfolio is flexible and diversified, the headlines are just part of the story.

Buy individual investments, not market trends or economic forecasts. Like Warren Buffett and Coca-Cola, look for companies that are selling at a reasonable price and who have a good outlook, regardless of economy or unforeseen events. Buy the company, keep informed to make sure your original assumptions are correct, and hold it for the long-term.

CHAPTER SEVEN

Learning the Trade
Stock Splits and Dollar Averages

"The first rule of compounding is to never interrupt it unnecessarily." ~ Charlie Munger

Imagine that you came over to my house for dessert. Now imagine that I brought out a pecan pie. Or peanut butter pie. (It can be any flavor you choose, as long as you can imagine wanting a large piece.)

There are four of us sitting around the table, so I cut the pie into four equal portions.

Just before I serve the pieces of pie on the plates, I say, "You know, actually, I've decided that tonight, as a special occasion, everyone can have two pieces." Imagine you get all excited because you're so excited to have a double portion.

Then, you watch me cut that same pie into eight equal, smaller pieces. Sure enough, I give everyone two pieces. Yes, you have two pieces, but each piece is only half of the original piece.

When I set your plate before you, you would think, "What? Why? What's this about? There's no more than there was a moment ago." And you would be correct.

Just because I made it *sound* like you were getting twice the amount of pie doesn't mean that's the case. The size of the piece has changed, but the serving is the same. The nature of equivalent fractions means that you really got the exact same amount I offered in the first place.

You and I both know that 1/4 of the pie is the same fraction as 2/8 of the pie.

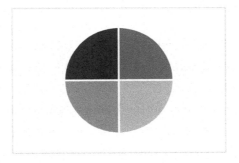

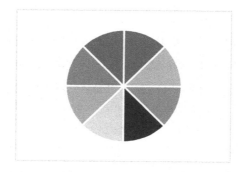

If that sounded like a word problem from fifth grade, then you're likely more familiar with the nature of stock splits than you thought. The media likes to play out a stock split as a big thing, but they are hoping you'll forget what your fifth-grade teacher taught you about fractions. They're cutting the same amount into smaller, equal pieces, and it really has no financial consequence to you, whatsoever.

Let's say that Giant Company is selling stock at $1,000 per share, and you have ten shares. You have $10,000 worth of assets in this company.

They announce a 10-for-1 **Stock Split**. Each share has split into ten, and the value per share has gone down from $1,000 to $100 per share. Your shares just multiplied by ten, so you now have one hundred shares. However, the price of the share has been divided by ten, so each share is worth $100.

What does that mean to you? It means you still have $10,000 worth of assets in this company.

10 (1,000) = 100 (100).

It's all $10,000, no matter how you slice it.

The media often makes it sound like stock splitting is a financial windfall, but it's not. They cut the same pie into smaller equal pieces, but the amount is no more than it was before.

The main reason that a company decides to split their stock is to become a small-investor friendly. Giant Company. The average investor can purchase a share at $100, where maybe they could not when it was $1,000 per share. Stock splits are in favor of the small investor – it makes the investment attainable for someone who doesn't have as much to invest on hand.

But also, it's a little bit of a mental game. It's the same slice of pie.

We can break that down even further, into what is called **Stock Slices**, where brokerage firms will allow you to purchase percentages of a share. Essentially, they'll allow you to buy "a fraction of a fraction." This option didn't exist five years ago, so it's a relatively new concept that has been part of the democratization of finance. What was once only available to the wealthiest of people is now available to anyone with a little extra cash.

Stock Split

When a company splits its shares to create more purchasing opportunities for new shareholders, existing shareholders maintain their share in proportion to their current holdings. It sounds like more money, but the proportion stays the same.

Stock Slices

Instead of purchasing a whole share of stock, you can purchase a fraction of a share for as little as $5.

Dollar Cost Averaging

Dollar Cost Averaging used to mean one thing, and now it has evolved over time to mean something different. Each concept is a long-term strategy, and each one depends on the individual's risk tolerance.

Let's look at the first concept, and let's say you have a lump sum of money. Maybe you win the lottery or acquire a sizeable inheritance, but it kind of makes you a little bit nervous to drop it all into the market at once. You might not feel especially confident to put $1.2 million dollars into the market all in one day, even though you have that much money at your disposal. You know the market fluctuates, and you know it could go up or down dramatically the very next day.

With Dollar Cost Averaging, a person might decide to invest $100,000 this month, then $100,000 next month, $100,000 the next month, and so on until you have invested 1.2 million dollars over the course of a year. With this method, considering whatever the market does over the course of a year or more, you're averaging up or averaging down over that period of time. You're not risking all your money in one big decision, but rather the average of many smaller decisions.

Now, the truth of the matter is this: that method is profitable only one-third of the time. (The second third of the time, the method loses money, and in the last third of the time, the method stays the same.) Only 1/3 of the time will you make more money by spreading your investment out, rather than by putting it all in the market at one time.

(If this is your comfort level, then it might be the best path for you.)

Imagine this with me. If you had 1.2 million dollars and you invested it all in one day, then by the end of the year you might have 2 million dollars. However, in the months in between, it may have dipped down to $700,000 in a bear market or market correction. These things don't happen every year, but they do happen on occasion—like in Y2K, in the financial crisis of 2008, and in the pandemic. Imagine what that was like for the people who had invested the Friday before the market dropped, October 19, 1987, 22.6% drop.

This is where being honest about your risk tolerance comes into play, and this is where you should ask yourself: would that ride be too stressful for me?

People who are new at investing – or misjudged their tolerance – would probably panic and sell. But those who held onto it would fare better in the end.

Remember, over the long run the market is always trending up. Other than the short corrections or longer bear markets, the market is always moving up. This way of "timing the market" does not average out in your favor. Still, it may feel like the best choice for someone who has a lower risk tolerance. Even if it doesn't make financial sense, and even if the odds aren't in their favor, this kind of averaging may make them more comfortable.

Invest Now

We cannot make every decision simply by counting dollars and cents. We have to weigh in your emotions, psychological aspects, and realize that each individual is different. None of these rules are perfect for everyone.

This is the Human Element. We start with an algorithm, and it's fairly accurate. But things happen that can alter the course of what we're expecting. This is the Human Element of investing, the part that is linked to personal emotions, preferences, and instincts.

Incremental Investing

The second concept of Dollar Cost Averaging is one that I actually like more: **Incremental Investing.** When you incrementally invest, you're putting a little away at a time, like in a 401(k), or a budget to set aside a certain amount each month.

Let's say we decide to put this money into an S&P 500 **ETF.**

The first month, the stock is selling at $10 a share. When we put our $100 in the market, we can purchase ten shares.

The second month, it fell by 50%, so the stock is selling at $5 a share. (Movements like this are not realistic or literal. This is just to bring the point home.) When we put our $100 in the market, we can buy twenty shares.

The third month, the stock goes all the way up to $20 a share. When we put our $100 in the market, we can buy five shares.

Over the course of three months, you didn't buy them all at the top of the market, but you didn't buy them all at the bottom, either. You bought each share for between $5 and $20, which means the dollar cost average is $11.50 each.

Over time, this will help you compound your money. This is systematic investing. You don't start with a lump sum, but you start putting small amounts of money away each month, and it builds and builds over the course of time.

(Yet another reason to start investing today, even if it is a small bit at a time. The averages work in your favor.)

These two concepts of Dollar Cost Averaging are very different, but each one caters to the individual person's risk tolerance.

What Could This Be Worth Someday?

This is the number one question I get in my office, day in and day out. How much money will I have, and how fast will my money grow? What will this be worth someday? Everybody wants to know.

The answer depends on many factors, including how much time you have and how much risk you can handle, and we will talk about those elements in the chapters to come. Once we clarify how much risk you can navigate, we can then determine how aggressive you'd like to be with your portfolio – usually this brings

Rule of 72
A popular calculation tool to quickly estimate the number of years required for an investment will double in value.

us to an annual rate of return somewhere between 6-8%. Now we have some numbers to put into a simple formula that's easier than you might think.

The **Rule of 72** is a simple formula that estimates the number of years it will take for your investment to double.

$$Years\ to\ double = \frac{72}{Interest\ Rate}$$

72 divided by 6 is 12. A portfolio with 6% return rate will double every twelve years.

$$\frac{72}{6} = 12$$

72 divided by 8 is 9. A portfolio with an 8% return rate will double every nine years.

$$\frac{72}{8} = 9$$

So, let's say a guy brings a million dollars into my office, and we have determined that he can probably handle about a 6% rate of return in his portfolio, which means his money will grow 6% each year. I can divide his rate of return into 72, and the answer is 12. His principal will double every 12 years. (To keep this simple, we are leaving out taxes and other variables.)

In 12 years, 1 million will be worth approximately 2 million.

In 24 years, it will double again to approximately 4 million.

In 36 years, it will double again to approximately 8 million.

Not bad, right?

If you dive deep into the formula and ask the mathematicians who figured it out, they'll tell you lots of fancy explanations about how the Rule of 72 calculates compound interest rates and inflation and long-erm effects of annual fees,[28] but we don't need to know all of the why before we can appreciate the brilliance of the Rule of 72. It's just a rule that works, it is what it is, the facts are the facts. This easy rule can make your planning simple, no matter where you are or what resources you have at your fingertips.

Let's say I meet with someone who is 35, and they plan to work until they are 65. They have a portfolio of $250,000, and their goal rate of return is 8%. The Rule of 72 says it will double every nine years, so their $250,000 will double three times in thirty years. By the time they retire, they'll have approximately two million dollars.

Let's say I have a young professional in my office, maybe 25 years old. She's got $10,000 that she's rolling from a 401(k) into an IRA. She tells me she's ready to be fairly aggressive with her portfolio, and we're going to aim for a 12% rate of return. She's got an early start in investing, and she's going to work until she's 65. That's forty years in the market.

The **Rule of 72** tells us that her portfolio is going to double every six years. So, what does that mean for the original ten thousand? In forty years, it will double a little less than 7 times.

By the time she is 31, her original $10,000 will have doubled to approximately $20,000.

By the time she is 37, her account will have doubled again to approximately $40,000.

By the time she is 43, her account will have doubled again to approximately $80,000.

By the time she is 49, her account will have doubled again to approximately $160,000.

By the time she is 55, her account will have doubled again to approximately $320,000.

By the time she is 61, her account will have doubled again to approximately $640,000.

And nearing her retirement, her account will have doubled once more to approximately $1.2 million dollars.

Because she has invested in a ROTH IRA, it's all <u>tax free</u>. (More on that in the retirement chapters!)

These are powerful examples I use in meetings, especially with people in their 20s, 30s, 40s. Those numbers are pretty motivating for anyone, especially young people looking at a long career where they can map out such a reality. Then I remind them, "Imagine if you added $100 to that every month. This number will go up dramatically." Dividends, Compound Interest, and the Rule of 72—these are the powerful tools that can transform your retirement into years you can enjoy.

Don't let your emergency fund get too big. I worked with a client who had $300,000 sitting in a savings account, where it could earn .03%. (That's one-third of one percent.) With the rate of inflation at 6%, they were losing 5.7% of their own money. In a situation like that, a savings account is not in your best interest, and you've let your emergency fund grow too big. We're going to move the bulk of it into a brokerage account, where—even if we're being conservative—it will grow by at least 3%.

Create a Plan. Now that you know what you want, listing your most important goals first, consider how many years you have to meet each specific goal. When you save or invest, you'll need to find an option that fits your time frame. Create a savings and investment plan based on your goals and pay off high-interest debt first. Participate in your company's 401(k) plan and max out any employer match. Research all investments thoroughly. Understand your risk tolerance, which we will discuss in the next chapter.

Stay the Course. If you were traveling from Maine to Washington, you would know your destination. You would set your plan, map your travel days, and stay your course. You probably wouldn't just wander off down an exit that you know nothing about, just to feel your way along the route from Maine to Washington. That kind of impulsive decision would add extra nights, extra fuel, extra meals, and extra cost. Make too many of those decisions, and you could derail your trip completely. It's best to stay the course.

Contrarian
The Individual who believes that the popular trends are always wrong, and therefore seeks opportunities to invest against the prevailing trend

In the same way, and in keeping with our travel analogy, stay the course. It is not wise to wander down an unknown investment path that you know nothing about, just to feel your way along the route to retirement. Impulsive decisions can lead to unnecessary mistakes.

85

Instead, once you have identified your risks, your tolerance, and your best path, stay the course – and stay in your lane.

Don't Chase the Crowd

There is a trend among investors in the stock market to get swept into herd mentality, which is the tendency of people in a group to think and behave in ways that conform with others in the group, rather than to think as individuals.

This has become even more common with the rising use of social media and stock bulletin boards, as these sources breed a sense of FOMO: Fear of Missing Out. When we see people flocking to make the same decision in response to market shifts, we begin to wonder if they know something we don't know. But this is exactly the time when we need to resist emotional responses.

While nobody knows with certainty which way the markets are going to go, in the short term, it's usually wise to avoid following the herd. This is one axiom that tends to hold true over time.

Trust me on this, our friends at the Fourth of July barbeque, our family at a niece's birthday party, and the collective drunk uncles at the holiday potluck do not have the inside scoops on the hottest trends. When the internet and media sites are reporting on "the hot trend" or giving you "latest and greatest stock tip," the news has already been reflected in the price of the security or sector. By the time the mass of retail investors has caught on to a new fad, prices are likely too high, and the investment is overvalued. The latest trends become a risky choice.

Contrarian investing is a strategy of purchasing and selling in contrast to the popular trends of the day.[29] When everyone thinks a stock will do poorly, the contrarian has an opportunity to purchase distressed stocks and sell them after the company recovers, making excellent gains. In the same way, widespread hype for a specific stock can cause prices to go higher than they should, leading to dramatic drops when the results don't match the expectations. While contrarian investing isn't a foolproof strategy, it does present opportunities to buy and sell at the most effective times.

Back in the 1990s, investment clubs were a big deal. Club members would pool their money, research a few stocks, and then buy or sell based on the majority vote of the group. Researchers at the University of California conducted a study to measure the effect of Group Think on investors and their returns, and they found that the investment returns of clubs lagged the S&P 500 index by nearly 4 percent a per year.[30] In other words, investing in what is "hot" is likely to get you burned.

The "herd mentality" has been thoroughly studied and is one of the biggest mistakes individual investors make. Instead, we are wise to invest based on objective research, calculated choices, a realistic assessment of risk, and a rugged determination to avoid emotional decisions.

CHAPTER EIGHT

What is At Stake?
Identify Your Risks

A wise man thinks ahead; a fool doesn't, and even brags about it! -- Proverbs 13:16

When we compare the financial paths of those who invest and those who do not, we can see the benefits are many. So, if the benefits are so many, why isn't everyone investing?

The answer comes down to one word: **Risk**. Not everybody can tolerate the risks involved with investing money.

Perhaps you feel like you're ready to sign up for an aggressive approach to growing your investments. Or, perhaps you prefer a more measured approach, and maybe you're most comfortable with little risk at all. There are no wrong answers with risk tolerance; there is only what is right for you. The important tasks are figuring out what you prefer, what you can tolerate, and what is best for your financial future.

Let's be honest: it's mostly about discipline and education. There are risks inherent to any venture, and a wise person will learn as much as they can before they begin. By reading this book, you have already taken a step toward the education, preparation, and understanding you need.

In this chapter we will identify the risks of investing. Let's begin with the most silent risk of all: the Risk of Doing Nothing.

The Risk of Doing Nothing

If you've recently come into some money, it may feel safest to put the money in a savings account to keep it safe and sound. You might think, "Isn't that the safest place for it? I mean, I'm not spending it if it's tucked away in there. I'll get a monthly statement to show me all the commas and zeroes, and nothing can happen to my money while it's tucked safely in the bank."

This is "risk of doing nothing," and it is the quietest risk of all. If your money sits in a bank account, or tucked into an envelope under your mattress, the dollars may stay the same, yes. But the value will depreciate dramatically.

Inflation

An overall rise in the prices of goods, usually due to an increase in the volume of money. When there is a decrease in the purchasing power of money, the prices of goods and services rise.

Invest Now

The general shift in prices over time is a process called **inflation.** We might think it's a natural process; like children grow taller, prices increase over time. But inflation is actually an intentional process created by federal reserve banks when they create money and increase the monetary supply. Our currency is devalued by our central bank, also known as the Fed, every year. In the century since the U.S. Department of Labor began tracking prices, the annual inflation rate has been 3.22 percent per year. What does that mean to you and me? It means that what our grandparents could buy for one dollar in 1913 will cost us nearly $24 today. You've heard the saying, "Don't spend it all in one place," and that rule becomes harder and harder to abide with each passing year

You might think inflation is price tags creeping up over time, but the process is far closer to ruining a cup of coffee.

Imagine if I placed before you the world's most perfect cup of coffee. A steaming blend of roasted beans, a nutty and caramel aroma, a cup of java prepared just for you. I invite you to take a sip, and you nod in agreement: that's a good cup of coffee.

But before you take another sip, I bring to the table a silver kettle of hot water that's been boiling on the stove. I start pouring that hot water into your coffee.

It's an ingredient that's already in your cup, so I'm only adding more of what you already have, right? But too much water will turn that perfect cup of coffee into a diluted cup of caffeine that won't carry you halfway through the morning.

A person who doesn't understand the ratio of coffee beans and water would say you could just add more water. But a coffee connoisseur wouldn't want you to mess with their ratios.

In the same way, some people might suggest that we could just print more money to make up for what we've spent. Let's just get some more of the ingredients we already have. But as the government prints more and more money to cover its spending every year, the value of the dollar is diluted just like that once-perfect cup of coffee.

As more money exists in the economy, the value decreases. The devaluation of currency turns that same dollar into something that won't sustain its purchasing power.

Less than a century ago, our grandparents paid about $0.23 for a gallon of milk in the 1930s. The average hourly wage was $0.30 an hour, and the average annual income for a household was $1,368. They could buy a car for around $750 and a house for about $4,000.00.[31]

Hyperinflation

When prices increase rapidly and out-of-control over a short amount of time. Hyperinflation can happen in times of war and economic turmoil, especially when a central bank prints an excessive amount of money.

We look at those numbers today, and it seems crazy to imagine prices like that.

When we go to the grocery store now, we pay anywhere from $3.00 - $7.00 for a gallon of milk, depending on the brand and the source.[32] The average hourly wage is approaching $25.66[33] as I write this, and the median household income is $67,788.[34] What our grandparents could buy for $20.00 would now cost us more than $235.00.[35]

If that kind of change happened in a short period of time, a process called **hyperinflation**,[36] everybody would notice. But the gradual decrease of the purchasing power dollar is almost imperceptible from year to year. That's why it feels safest to do nothing, to put that money in a savings account or under a mattress. How much could it change from year to year?

The answer is, not much. But over time, it will decrease dramatically. One dollar today won't get you as much as it did a decade ago, and it will buy even less one decade from now.

We are dealing with greater inflation rates for the first time again since the 1980s. In the Spring of 2022, it was running over 7%. That means at the end of one year, your $100 is now worth $93. Multiply that by three years, and you're down to less than $80. The purchasing power of money trickles away when you do nothing with it.

While it may feel emotionally safer to keep your money tucked in a savings account, you're losing 7% each year if you let it sit in the bank at today's inflation rate. Low risk investments tend to generate low rates of return, and sometimes those low rates may fail to keep pace with inflation. That's the risk of doing nothing; if you don't invest in *something,* you're losing money every day.

This is the risk of doing nothing. And it's definitely not the only risk.

Liquidity Risk

Perhaps you've received a postcard in your mailbox, glossy and impressive, inviting you to a free steak dinner at a fancy restaurant near you. These people will buy your dinner and talk to you about an "amazing" investment opportunity that will pay off in amazing dividends for your "amazing" retirement. The whole thing sounds "*amazing.*"

Let me tell you what will happen at that dinner: some people in expensive suits are going to invite you to invest in a very large housing complex, downtown skyscraper, or perhaps even your local grocery-anchored strip mall. They'll make it sound polished and exciting, like there's no way you lose. You'll be tempted to sign up. I get it.

Money talks. So does the free wine that comes with the steak.

But here's the catch: a word called **liquidity.**[37] Liquidity is your ability to access your invested money.

Consider the nature of liquid, the scientific properties that define it. Liquids take the shape of the container they are in, they have a definite volume, and—most importantly in the context of this conversation—the particles of the liquid are free to *move*. In similar terms, a liquid investment (or a liquid asset) can quickly

> **Liquidity**
>
> *The ability to convert an asset into cash when you need it. The easier it is for an asset to turn into cash, the more liquid it is. Cash is the most liquid of assets, followed by stocks and bonds.*

and easily be converted to cash. When you need to spend it, you can. The money is yours to *move* as you choose.

If you make the investment they present to you at most steak dinner sales pitches, you will likely lose your liquidity. Your money will be tied up for years to come. Rental and housing markets don't move fast, because you cannot sell a house or property overnight in most markets. Stocks take two days to settle, mutual funds take one day. They are liquid investments you can access, because when you need money, you need it now.

There's a risk with the property investment—even with the steak dinner included—that your money won't come back to you for a long, long time, if ever. Many of these investments never repay your principal in a lump sum but rather in monthly or quarterly installments over many, many years.

The Risk of Procrastination

Most people agree that investing is a good idea, but most people choose to put it off until next month or next year. When they get a raise or some extra cash on hand, it's tempting to spend that money on a special something, to add the money into the budget as disposable income, or to get the next vacation written in ink on the calendar.

The younger a person is, the more immortal they feel. This leads young people to believe they can always start saving "later." It's tempting to procrastinate planning your financial future, but your thirties soon become your forties, and your forties spill right into your fifties with a few more trips around the sun. Your money could have multiplied in all those years. The risk of procrastination makes you think you have more time to make your money work for you.

"Someday" only happens if you act today.

If you delay your financial plan, you'll miss out on the most powerful tool, compound interest, and the toll of those days, months or years of not getting started can add up to missing out on some great gains. If you wait too long to enter the market at all, your procrastination could have a larger impact than you realize.

Remember, you don't need *to time the market* to make your funds grow. **You need time *in the market*.**

The Risk of False Perception

Risk perception is the individual verdict any of us might make about the nearness of danger. Our brains are always measuring the risks of any decision, and our perceptions become our reality. It is the perceived, unknown risks that make simple decisions more difficult than they need to be.

Before a person might go swimming, he might check the weather report for any incoming rain or thunderstorms. He might count how many lifeguards are on duty before he takes his children into the water. He might scan the horizon for shark fins. He's measuring the risks based on the information he has.

Our risk perceptions are affected by many things – our current emotions, our personal history, and our intake of new information through our various avenues of media. So, if this guy is planning to take his kids swimming, but he just finished *Shark Week* on Animal Planet, he may have a much higher perception of shark fins in the waters. The truth is, there may be no sharks for miles around, but he can imagine them circling their prey: his children.

They're probably not going swimming that day. The perceived risk is high.

Sometimes fears are legitimate, and sometimes they are manufactured by those factors: our emotions, history, and the media we're watching. A few years ago, I received a frantic phone call from a client – from underneath her coffee table. She was watching the financial report on the news, she was crying and terrified, afraid she had lost everything, and calling me to confirm her financial doom.

As far as I know, that's the first and only time someone has called me from underneath the protection of a piece of living room furniture.

My first advice to her was this: Turn off the TV. This is not a good resource for your daily financial advice, and their panic machines had driven her to edge of a breakdown.

Second, and thankfully, her risks were only her perception. Yes, perception is reality, and what she thought and feared had spun her nearly into orbit. But the truth was, their portfolio was secure. I was able to talk her back into peace of mind – and out from under the table.

The Risk of Comparison

Not so long ago, when cocktail parties were a cultural pastime and neighbors loved to gather at each other's homes for evening spirits, there was a tendency for people to chat about their stock ventures, their greatest new investments, and their slice of pie in the sky. Today, we might not see this happening as much at cocktail parties, but we'll see it in the pervasive personal competitions of social media.

"Keeping up with the Joneses" is a pattern fueled by comparisons, and we can get misled by someone else's image management. They might post a picture of the new car they purchased with their windfall in the market, and that green monster of envy and curiosity might whisper to you, "Wait a minute. Where did he get that tip? What is he investing in? What don't I know? How can I get in on this?" You might feel tempted to take stock tips from people who aren't qualified to give such information, and the risk of social pressures can take you and your financial future down a dangerous path.

Joshua Brown is the CEO of a successful wealth management company, the author of multiple books, and the creator of a widely read blog, The Reformed Broker. His company manages billions for individual investors, corporations, and foundations. He writes, "One major life lesson I've learned over the years is to never argue the merits of my own portfolio with anyone else. There will always be people who criticize how others invest and what they invest in, but these arguments are usually coming from a place of insecurity and doubt. If you're confident in what you're doing, then the last thing in the world you're worried about is what other people are doing.... Worry about your own portfolio and I'll focus on my own."[38]

Stay in your lane, follow your financial plan, and know your own goals. None of these should be affected by anybody else's financial choices.

The Risk of Missing the Best Days in the Market

We have talked about turning off the noise of network financial news, since that kind of brain clutter can breed fear and emotional decisions. Remember, those news reports are not in your best interest, and sometimes they make announcements to intentionally scare you, the individual investor. Institutions will shake the tree, so to speak, to frighten the ones who aren't strong enough to hold on through an impending storm.

This is so common, in fact, we have a kind of "informal market indicator" in our practice that has proven to be consistent. When the market takes a dip, phone calls start coming in. People watch the news, they monitor the fluctuations, they get nervous—and they pick up the phone and call our office. We might get a dozen calls from investors—sometimes more than that. The institutions are shaking the trees, scaring the individual investors to pull out of the market. Every time we get that flurry of phone calls, with the panic rising higher and higher, we know we are reaching the end of the downturn. When those phone calls reach a frenzied level, we know we can expect the market to rebound soon—and often very soon. This informal measurement of investor sentiment has served us very well for more than twenty-five years. In fact, it worked great again in June of 2022. Since the peak of chaos, the market was up as much as 16 percent over the next six weeks.

Some people get so nervous about avoiding the bad days in the market, that they withdraw their money to protect the cash. But here's the mathematical truth about the markets: the market always, always, *always* recovers with time. A bad period is always followed by a good period. If you pull out in fear during the bad days, you will miss the best days, too.

We cannot predict when the market will take its next dip nor how long it will last, but if you pull out during the drop, you're likely to miss the rebound as well. Missing even just a few of the market's best days of recovery can affect your portfolio's overall return.

I worked with a couple who asked me to manage their individual retirement accounts. (This happens more and more often, partners investing in separate accounts.) As the economy and the markets crashed in 2008, the husband and wife had two very different approaches with their money: He kept his money in the market, while she panicked, sold her investments, and went to all cash. She wanted to avoid the bad days of the market.

On the surface, it may seem harmless—even wise—to avoid the bad days, but this also means missing the good days that are sure to come.

The couple started with the same amount of money invested, but their financial plans followed two very different courses. The husband kept his money in the market. He took the hit when the markets were down, but his money was still in the market when it recovered. The wife, on the other hand, didn't give her money the chance to recover, and she missed the first few years of rebound in the market.

If I showed you their accounts today, you would see that his numbers have more than doubled hers. That's the benefit of time in the market.

Studies published by both JP Morgan and Putnam Investments have shown similar results. In their example an initial investment of $10,000 could grow to $29,845 over the course of twenty years, if the investor stayed invested every day, no matter the market conditions.

If the investor missed the ten best days, their dollar value would but cut in half, down to $14,895.

If the investor missed the twenty best days, their dollar value would drop down to $9,359.

If the investor missed the thirty best days, their dollar value would drop to $6,213.

If the investor missed the forty best days, their dollar value would drop to $4,241.

If the investor missed the fifty best days, their dollar value would drop to $2,985.

If the investor missed the sixty best days, their dollar value would drop to $2,144.[39]

The average daily percent move of the stock market increases over time, so an initial investment of $10,000 could grow to $29,845 over the course of twenty years, if the investor stayed invested.

The return went from positive to negative by missing the 20 best days of the market over 20 years. Putnam Investments found similar results by studying the data from 2003 to 2018. If you were fully invested in the S&P 500, your annualized total return was 7.7% during that time. But if you missed the 10 best days in the market, it dropped to a paltry 2.65%. (SOURCE: JP MORGAN.)

The best days follow the worst days, but the best days can't be predicted. As you can see, you don't have to miss many good days to feel the impact. It adds up quickly ... or, rather, subtracts quickly.

So then, how does one navigate the good and the bad? Stay in the market—to the level of the risk you can personally tolerate.[1] In the next chapter, we will discuss some tools to determine the level of risk is right for you.

---

[1] Many of the best days in the market come right after the worst days. According to the J.P. Morgan study, six of the 10 best days occurred within two weeks of the 10 worst days. One example was in 2015: The best day was Aug. 26, just two days after the worst day in the stock market that year.

CHAPTER NINE

What Can You Handle?
Measure Your Risk Tolerance

*"How many millionaires do you know who have become
wealthy by investing in savings accounts? I rest my case.
"* — Robert G. Allen,
(Author of *Multiple Streams of Income:
How to Generate a Lifetime of Unlimited Wealth)*

Every investment decision involves a degree of risk, and each
investor handles risk differently. Market volatility can be
extremely stressful for some people, while others take the ups and
downs in stride. Factors such as how fast you can get your money
when you need it, how quickly your money will grow, and how
safe your money will be – all of these can affect how well you
sleep at night, knowing your money is in good hands.

Risk Tolerance is your personal capacity to manage the possibilities and probabilities of investing. Truly, you probably won't know your own risk tolerance until you invest some money and encounter fluctuations in the market. You'll discover how aggressive you want to be during your first stock market rally, and how nervous you feel when the stock market is falling. Sometimes we don't know what we want and need until we are faced with the actual problem to solve. Your risk tolerance is based on your individual comfort level, considering the following factors:

Your Age: Young investors should be able to take more risks than older investors. Time is on their side, and they often have the capacity to continue working and generating income alongside their investments. You can take more risks when you are younger, because your retirement is still likely far away. Older investors are closer to retirement, and they don't have as much time to recover if their investments take a hit.

Your Timeline: Do you need a certain sum of money in five years, or can you let it grow for fifteen years? Generally, you can take more risks if you have more time. The market continues on an upward trend over the years, which can allow you to take risks and recover if the market doesn't go the way you had planned.

Your Goals: Some people want to invest so they can accumulate the highest amount of money possible, but others have saved a great amount of money and they do not need to generate more money than they could never spend. Some people are investing to grow, others are investing to maintain. Each person's goals are unique. Knowing what you want your money to do will affect the risks you want to take.

The Size of Your Portfolio: Sometimes people have more than they need or ever anticipated having. If so, you may be more tolerant to risk since a drop in the market is less likely to result in a life-altering decline. Depending on the needs of a particular investor an individual with a $20 million portfolio may be able to take more risk than an investor with a $2 million portfolio. On the other hand, the investor with just $500 thousand may need to have a much larger portfolio to meet their needs and must take more risk to meet their goals. (These are big numbers, and you don't have to have this kind of portfolio in order to be a successful investor—so please don't be discouraged. I toss these out there because it is possible to see some big numbers when you let your money do the work, and you can only get these numbers if you start somewhere.)

For example, consider Carol and James, a mother and son, each with their own portfolio. Carol is a retiree who lives in Fort Lauderdale. Her pension is $3,000 per month, and she has invested $10,000 in savings bonds that will mature in fifteen years, giving her extra income after the age of 75. Carol does not like investment risk, and she has chosen a safe and predictable path as a conservative investor.

James is 32 years old, a successful young professional and already a cultured investor. He has a highly diversified portfolio with stocks, CDs, and mutual funds, and he's aggressive with his trading. James is a short-term investor, always looking to gain the maximum return over three to six months. If the market takes a turn, his diverse portfolio—and potentially long career ahead of him—will allow him to recover.

Carol and James have each made wise decisions with their investments, based on their goals, timeline, and personal tolerance for risks.

Invisible Factors that Affect Your Risk Tolerance

New research has shown that the human tolerance for risk has some invisible factors as well, and these relate directly to personality traits.[40] If you are someone who often experiences **regret**, if you tend to look back and second-guess decisions, then your risk tolerance may fluctuate. You may worry you have taken too much risk, or you may kick yourself later as others make more money than you do.

Some people lean toward **overconfidence**, feeling better about their decisions than they truly should. Overconfidence can be a blind spot, a personal weakness we often cannot see in ourselves. Why? Ironically, it's because we feel too confident to believe it could happen to us. These people may take on more risk than they should.

Other people are perpetually **optimistic**, believing everything will forever turn out for the best. Optimism is a wonderful trait in a person, but realism is a smarter trait in the financial markets. If you hope your investments will soar to the moon and beyond in a short amount of time, your optimism may make you overly aggressive.

Your Risk Tolerance

Let's address the real questions that pertain to you and your future, your individual level of risk tolerance, and how much you are willing to tolerate. We can measure your individual score with a balance of questions that focus on objective facts and subjective preferences. These will measure your risk tolerance, whether you are someone who can handle the volatility, or someone who hates to take any chances.

Answer the following questions to measure your personal risk profile. Don't give the answer you wish you could give, and don't give the answer you hope will be true. Answer the questions with honesty and self-awareness and score your points in the margin.

1. How old are you?
   - Over 65 years old   (1)
   - 55-64 years old   (2)
   - 45-54 years old   (4)
   - 30-44 years old   (6)
   - 18-29 years old   (8)

2. What are your primary goals?
   - Retirement
   - Wealth accumulation

- Paying down debt
- College savings
- Income

3. When do you plan to retire?
   - I am already retired. (0)
   - I plan to retire in 1-5 years. (1)
   - I plan to retire in 6-10 years. (3)
   - I plan to retire in 11-20 years. (6)
   - I have many years ahead of me, and I plan to retire in 20 or more years. (8)

4. When do you plan to begin withdrawing funds from your investment accounts?*
   - 1-5 years (1)
   - 6-10 years (3)
   - 11-15 years (6)
   - 16 or more years (8)

5. If you suddenly lost your income, for how many months could you continue to pay all your living expenses from existing cash and cash equivalents?
   - Less than one month (0)
   - 2-3 months (2)
   - 4-6 months (4)
   - More than 6 months (6)

Invest Now

6. Many experts suggest that you should plan as though you will live into your nineties. With this suggestion in mind, how long do you anticipate being retired?

- 1-5 years   (1)
- 6-10 years   (3)
- 11-20 years   (6)
- 21 or more years   (8)

7. There is a general increase in prices over time, and the value of money goes down as the prices increase. With this in mind, which statement best reflects your attitude toward taking a risk in order to maintain the equivalent value of your money as the economy grows and inflates?

- I want to avoid risk, no matter the effect of inflation. (2)
- I am willing to assume a moderate level of risk in an effort stay ahead of inflation.   (3)
- I am willing to accept a substantial level of risk in an effort to significantly outpace inflation.   (6)

8. As you monitor the performance of your portfolio, which of the following concerns you the most?

- Not meeting expected **returns**   (6)
- Long-term erosion of **principal**   (2)
- Short-term fluctuation in portfolio value (4)
- Not keeping up with inflation   (3)

9. Which statement best describes how you feel about fluctuations in the value of your portfolio?

- I have no tolerance for **fluctuations**.   (1)
- I feel somewhat uncomfortable with fluctuations. (3)
- Fluctuations do not bother me.   (6)

10. Would you rather have someone give you a check for $500 right now, or would you pass up that gift if they gave you a 50% chance of it growing into $2,000? What would you choose? (There is no right or wrong answer.)

- Give me the $500 today.   (2)
- I'll pass on the $500 for a chance to make $2,000, knowing I might make zero.   (4)

Add some zeroes to that equation, and let's consider it again. Would you rather have $50,000 right now, or a 50% chance at $200,000? Again, there is no right or wrong answer, but in this case, many people will second-guess the risk and potential of the larger amount. After all, $50,000 is already a large amount of money. What would you choose?

- Give me the $50,000 today.   (4)
- I'll pass on the 50,000 for the chance at 200,000, knowing I might make zero.   (8)

Consider these two investment options, each with growth, but with different risk patterns.

Invest Now

Investment A has a higher risk with greater growth, a great drop, and then it lands on top with a positive return after five years. Investment B has a slower growth, a small drop. It grows steadily upward, but at the end of five years, the return is not as high.

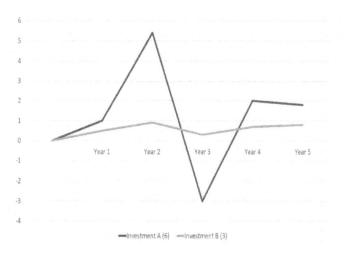

Consider how you would feel about these returns. Would you be more uncomfortable to see the giant drop, or less growth overall?

Investment A   (6)

Investment B   (3)

11.You bought a growth stock investment about one year ago, and you heard on the evening news that the stock dropped 10% overnight. What are you most inclined to do?

- Sell the investment immediately. (1)
- Hold onto it and see what happens. (4)
- Buy more while the prices are lower. (6)

Well, how did you do? What is your total score?

0-18 Points: Lowest Risk Profile. You prefer to take little to no risk.

19-24 Points: Low Risk Profile. You are comfortable with a small amount of risk.

25-31 Points: Medium Risk Profile. You are prepared to take risk to see some growth.

32-37 Points: High Risk Profile. You have plenty of time to let your money grow and recover, so you are willing to take high risk.

38-45 Points: Highest Risk Profile. You are focused on growth, and you're willing to take aggressive risk for high rewards.

Measuring your risk tolerance level will help you to realistically manage your portfolio and make effective investment decisions alongside your financial planner.

Be honest with yourself. This is the most important guideline in measuring your risk tolerance. It may be easy to say,

"I can handle a high level of risk," but that may or may not be true. Consider carefully how much you can afford to lose, what you stand to gain, and how you personally tend to handle risk in your private life.

It may seem like it's a harmless miscalculation to wish you could handle more risk, but misinformation will not help either of us to manage your money effectively. When people aren't honest about their risk tolerance, they will inevitably end up in a situation that makes them uncomfortable—and neither of us wants that to happen.

When I have had a client who has inaccurately measured their risk tolerance, they get super nervous when we begin investing. They begin to discover that maybe they're not as comfortable with risk – or not as risk-adverse – as they thought. Sometimes we need to start from the beginning to re-evaluate the risk profile.

A skilled advisor knows more than just investments—they know their clients well enough to know what combination of investments will work for each person. If you're honest about what you can tolerate, then you should be able to ride through anything that comes up.

CHAPTER TEN

Planning Your Journey

"There's an old quip that personal finance is more personal than finance. Though perhaps too clever, this still reveals a truth only sparingly mentioned among serious financial experts: **There is no one right way to manage your money.***"*

-- Brian Portnoy, founder of *Shaping Wealth* and co-editor of the book, *How I invest My Money*

Now that we know your goals and we have identified your risk tolerance, we can consider the best options for the journey. Just as there are different vacation styles for every personality, and just as there are a dozen different ways to get to any destination. We can narrow down the options that best suit you.

I know many advisors who present their clients with a 30-page packet to wow and impress, but often that results in intimidation and overwhelm. It's not something the client is interested in reading, and they're going to throw it in the trash when they get home. It's too much.

Instead, I like to do what we call "back of envelope planning," meaning, I could literally write it on the back of an envelope. If we were sitting at a bar, I might write it on a cocktail napkin. The point is, if I can give you a few easy concepts to think about, then I give you something to work with.

An **investment portfolio** is an entire snapshot of your investments. While entire books are written on how to diversify and create a portfolio that best suits your needs, here we will keep our focus on the novice investor as we cover the basics, focusing on a portfolio of liquid investments.

Think of various assets classes as ingredients in a recipe that make up a pie. Stocks, bonds, and cash are the primary ingredients of a simple asset allocation model. Below are examples of the simplest allocation, simply stocks and bonds—call it the "mac and cheese" of this culinary tour.

These are very simple allocations, but they amply demonstrate the difference in return as you add more stock—which is also risk. Each ones shows the best- and worst-case scenarios, or increased volatility. The important thing is to notice how the average annual return increases along with the addition of risk, like adding a little spice until you get your favorite dish just right.

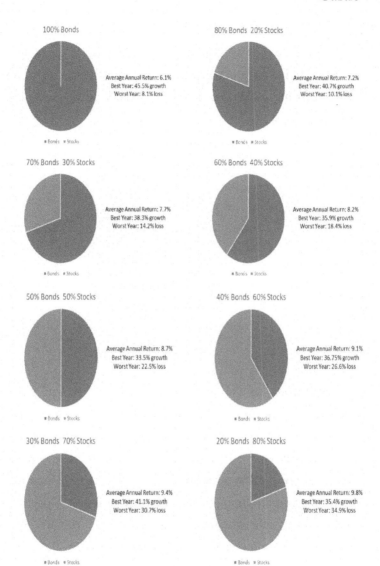

100% Bonds
Average Annual Return: 6.1%
Best Year: 45.5% growth
Worst Year: 8.1% loss

80% Bonds 20% Stocks
Average Annual Return: 7.2%
Best Year: 40.7% growth
Worst Year: 10.1% loss

70% Bonds 30% Stocks
Average Annual Return: 7.7%
Best Year: 38.3% growth
Worst Year: 14.2% loss

60% Bonds 40% Stocks
Average Annual Return: 8.2%
Best Year: 35.9% growth
Worst Year: 18.4% loss

50% Bonds 50% Stocks
Average Annual Return: 8.7%
Best Year: 33.5% growth
Worst Year: 22.5% loss

40% Bonds 60% Stocks
Average Annual Return: 9.1%
Best Year: 36.75% growth
Worst Year: 26.6% loss

30% Bonds 70% Stocks
Average Annual Return: 9.4%
Best Year: 41.1% growth
Worst Year: 30.7% loss

20% Bonds 80% Stocks
Average Annual Return: 9.8%
Best Year: 35.4% growth
Worst Year: 34.9% loss

Bonds Stocks

115

Each of these recipes will get the job done. They're each fine, and they will take the hunger away. But most of us like a few ingredients in our meals. A more common recipe – or portfolio – might look more like this balanced model below.

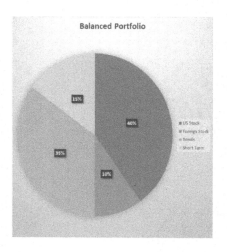

Still, some of us like our dishes even fancier and a little more complex. All of us that cook probably have that one ingredient we reach for, something that makes us yell "Pow!" as we drop it in the pan. In this case, the "Pow!" would be alternative investments.

Alternative Investments is an umbrella term that includes a wide range of assets like real estate, commodities, private equity, hedge funds, merger and acquisition funds, private equity, etc. Basically, alternatives include anything other than traditional stocks and bonds. Sure, U.S. stocks and bonds are included in a balanced portfolio, but these complex ingredients further diversify the dish and smooth out the flavor.

In recent years, we have seen alternative investments become mainstream. In fact, in the coming years, alternative investments are expected to grow from $13.9 billion in 2020 to $21.1 billion in 2025. Pow, indeed!

The impetus behind this projected growth is the belief that alternative investments enhance the risk/reward characteristics of a traditional stock and bond portfolio. That means lower volatility and higher returns.

A balanced portfolio with Alternative Investments might look like this.

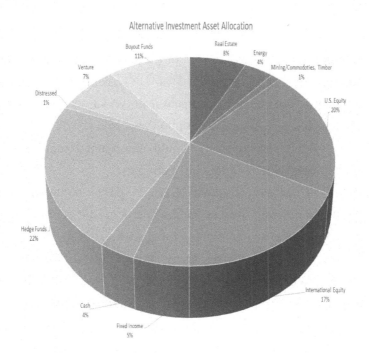

Alternative Investment Asset Allocation

So, what might your portfolio look like? Let's begin with what we have learned from your score.

Lowest Risk Profile – Expected Return 1-3%

If you scored 0-18 points on the Risk Tolerance Quiz, have the lowest risk profile, and your best plan is **Capital Preservation.** Essentially, our most important goal is to hold on to the money you have. Because preservation is the

Capital Preservation

Keeping your money safe with low-risk investments, instead of watching it grow with the chance of high risks.

paramount goal, we will be very conservative. This strategy is common among some retirees or those approaching retirement, as they may want to avoid loss at all costs. We are looking to safeguard your money, not make it grow, so our goal might be a 1% return on the cash you put into the account.

For this preference, I would recommend relatively "safe" investments, like the following examples:

Certificate of Deposit (CD): A CD is a savings account through a federally insured bank. You deposit a certain amount of money for a certain amount of time, such as six months, one year, or five years. In exchange, the bank pays interest for that amount of time. When you cash in your CD, you receive the money you originally invested, plus any interest that principal has accrued. This is a great choice for an investor with a low risk profile because the money is insured and expected to mature over a fixed amount of time.

Money Market Account: A money market account is another type of savings account, and it pays slightly higher interest back to you. This market grows from the daily and overnight swaps of funds between banks and economic institutions who lend money to one another. It can be a great place to park your money, as they pay a rate of return but should not go down in value.

Low Risk Profile

If you scored 19-24 points in the Risk Tolerance Quiz, you may be comfortable with some risk—but not very much. Your goal for your portfolio is both **Income and Preservation.** We would like to hold on to what you have, and we have a fairly short amount of time before your investment needs to mature. We can take a little bit of risk with the investments, allowing you to create some income with your cash. Keep your timeline in mind, and your goal might be a 3-5% return on the account.

The ingredients of this portfolio might include the following:

Short-Term Bond Fund: This is an investment product with maturity of less than five years, so the chance of loss is miniscule. The short-term bond invests in a portfolio of fixed-income securities, so the investor receives returns in the form of fixed periodic coupons. The risk is low, but the yield is also low.

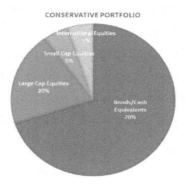

Medium Risk Profile

If you score 25-31 points on the Risk Tolerance Quiz, you are prepared to take some risk in order to see some conservative growth in your portfolio. Your timeline is ten years or more, giving your investment some time to navigate the highs and lows of the economy. We could aim for 4% to 6% optimal rate of return on your investments.

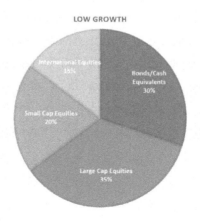

High-Risk Profile

If you score 32-37 points, you have a **High-Risk Profile.** You have plenty of time before you will need to access this money, so we can focus on **Growth and Income.** Time mitigates risk, and if the stock drops significantly, you'll have time for the market to recover before you'll need to dip into the fund. We can let this money grow as much as it can over the next thirty years, even if that means we might watch it swing as much as 20%. Over time, you'll get a much higher percentage, and we can aim for 6-8% rate of return.

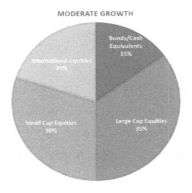

MODERATE GROWTH

If you scored 38 points or more, you have the **Highest Risk Profile,** and we can focus exclusively on **Growth** of the assets. We have plenty of time, ten years or more, so we don't have to worry about the ups and downs of short-term dips in the market. We want these assets to grow as much as they can over the next thirty years. We might see swings as much as twenty percent or even more, but in the long run and over time, you'll get a much higher percentage of growth.

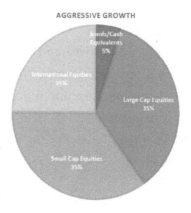

AGGRESSIVE GROWTH

Bonds/Cash Equivalents 5%

International Equities 25%

Large Cap Equities 35%

Small Cap Equities 35%

Measuring Performance

To assess how well your investments are doing, you'll need to consider several different ways of measuring performance. The measures you choose will depend on the information you're looking for and the types of investments you own. I'd like to invite you to measure your performance against your personal plan, not against the averages – and not against anyone else's performance.

Let's say you have a friend named Bob, and Bob is an investor with a different risk tolerance than you. Bob might say something like, "Hey, looks like the market is up 8%. Did you beat the market?"

And you might immediately think, "Oh, no. My portfolio only grew by 6%. We're not doing as well as we should."

Remember, *could* and *should* are not synonyms. They mean different things, and they travel in different lanes on the highway. Your car *could* travel at 120 mph, but that doesn't mean it *should.*

If your goal is to make 6% a year, based on the risk and return you are comfortable with, then you shouldn't care if the market is up 8%. Your goal is 6%. You met our goal.

If you happen to do more than 6% a year, then great – that will make up for the years when you do a little less.

Ultimately, you need to stay in your own lane. Tune out everyone else's money. Don't worry that Bob made 8% last year, because he may have taken some crazy risks to get there. Those same crazy risks might have given you an ulcer and too many sleepless nights. Whether you beat the market on a specific day is irrelevant to you as a personal investor.

Your goals are your guardrails, and they are based on you Risk Tolerance. If somebody else is making more money or "beating the market" faster than you, then remind yourself of your tolerance, your risks, and your goals. Your Risk Tolerance will tell you what lane to travel in, and your goals will keep you in your lane.

If you think of this as a race, then you'll always see someone who is ahead of you. But you don't know what their resources are, and you don't know how much they stand to lose. If you keep your own journey and your own goals in focus, then you can get where you intend to go.

Three Silent Predators: Taxes, Fees, and Inflation

Invest Now

Taxes, fees, and inflation are the three silent predators that quietly deplete your balances over time. Any investment strategy that fails to account for the effects of taxes, inflation, and fees will reduce your ability to increase your wealth over time. To maximize your investments over the long term, consider the effects of each one of these.

Taxes. While taxes are never the primary driver of any investment strategy, we would be foolish to ignore the efficiency of tax-deferred or tax-free accounts. If you are building assets in a regular brokerage or investment account, Uncle Sam will collect taxes on any capital gains, dividends, and additional income you receive. Keep tax efficiency in mind so that you get to keep more of what you earn.

Capital Gains
Profit from an investment

Dividends
Money paid regularly by a company to its shareholders

Income
Money received through work or investments

Inflation is the devaluation of our currency over time, resulting in higher prices on nearly everything. This is another powerful force that can eat away at your investment growth every year, as dollars have less and less purchasing power.

For example, let's say a candy bar cost 25 cents in 1975. At an average inflation rate of 4 percent, that same candy bar would cost about $1.30 in 2020. With much higher inflation rates in 2021 and 2022, that same candy bar is likely to cost $1.42 or more just two short years later. The dollar bill looks the same, but it doesn't pack the same punch.

Now, do that same math in the context of your investments, and you will see the damage done to your assets by the hidden tax of inflation. If you assume a 4 percent inflation rate, then the value of a $100,000 portfolio would be reduced to $67,500 in just ten years. That's an alarming decrease in purchasing power. Your investments would have to grow to $148,000 in that decade— that's 448 percent—simply to keep up with inflation. (And this does not include the effects of any additional taxes and fees.)

Fees. Fees seem simple enough: the lower the fees, the better right? I mean, there is a whole section of the financial industry telling us that the lower the fee the better off you will be, and to a certain extent, that is true... but not always. Just as with everything else in life, you get what you pay for.

The funds with the lowest fees are the most basic passive index funds. These fees could be .05 or even less. You are basically buying an index. There is nothing wrong with that, but it's a very basic, no-frills option. It's going to go up and down with the index.

An actively managed fund will cost more. Active funds might be 1.25 percent or higher in a mutual fund of .60-.85 in an ETF. They are researching and choosing stocks, which is very different from a passive index, so it costs more in staff and analysts to run the fund. Hopefully, for the higher fee you are getting a higher return and maybe less volatility.

Go a step further into liquid alternatives with far more complicated investment strategies, and your fee could easily be north of 2 percent. This fund may be a great diversifier to protect you greatly on the downside, so that fee could become valuable to you.

In the end, just like anything else in life, the cheapest route may not always be the best route.

Focus on the Total Return of Your Investments.

How do we navigate the quiet toll of inflation, taxes, and fees?

Invest in equities. Historically, common stocks have offered the best performance over time, proving to have the staying power to go the distance alongside inflation. From 1928 to 2011, the S&P 500 returned an average of 9.2 percent, while the Treasury bond returned just 5.1 percent and investment grade corporate bonds returned 6.0 percent. While it's riskier to invest in equities, that's where the money is. It's your armor to fight the effects of inflation.

If you are too conservative with your investments, by putting too much money in bonds that have a lower growth rate than inflation, you are likely falling behind over time. But if you can brave the volatility of the equity markets, you reduce the risk of running out of money later in life.

Take the Risk that is Right for You

How much risk is right for you? Excellent question. If you can get this answer right, you've accomplished the biggest part of your investment journey. I wish I could answer for you, but the decision is yours alone.

While nobody wants to lose money at any time, it is important to remember that over the long-run, higher risk means higher returns. At the same time, it's a balance. If we are too conservative, we may not reach our retirement goals, but if we are too risky, we may make irrational decisions that will lock in losses and derail the path to retirement all together. We each need to find the level of risk that we can live with when short-term corrections or other events affect the value of our investments. Knowing your risk tolerance will keep you from making an emotional decision at the wrong time. If you find you can't keep your emotions in check, then it's probably time to hire a professional advisor.

CHAPTER ELEVEN

What It Looks Like
A Story of Four Investors

"Important financial decisions are not made in spreadsheets or in textbooks. They are made at the dinner table. They aren't often made with the intention of maximizing returns but minimizing the chance of disappointing a spouse or child. Those kinds of things are difficult to summarize in charts or formulas, and they may vary widely from person to person. What works for one person may not work for another."

~ Morgan Housel, a partner at the Collaborative Fund and former columnist at *The Motley Fool* and *The Wall Street Journal*

Let's consider the paths of four investors. We can call them **Aware Alice, Procrastinator Paul, Keep-After-It Kate, and Traveler Tom.**

All four investors are the same age, they enter the workforce at the same time. Let's imagine they earn the same salary, and they each have the same budget to work with over their lifetime. Each one of them sets aside $1200 to invest per year, but they do so at different times in their lives, and the results are dramatically different.

Aware Alice

Our friend Alice starts investing at age 18, setting aside $100 a month to invest $1,200 per year. She keeps this pattern for ten years, ultimately investing a total of $12,000 in that decade between age 18 and age 28. The money grew to $18,344. At age 28, Alice gets married, and she decides to restructure the budget to purchase a home and grow a family. Alice always intends to come back to that old habit of setting aside $100 a month, but kids are expensive with endless needs, and Alice never builds that investment margin back into the budget. However, Alice doesn't touch the money they invested during those first ten years. She let that original decade's worth of $12,000 compound for forty years. With a rate of 8%, the money can grow considerably over time.

At age 38, her nest egg grew to $39,603.

At age 48, her nest egg grew to $85,501.

At age 58, her nest egg grew to $184,589.

And by the time Alice is ready to retire at age 68, the money has grown to more than $398,000. Ultimately, Alice put money into the account for only ten years, but with the power of compound interest and the strength of longevity, this original investment grew to just under $400,00.

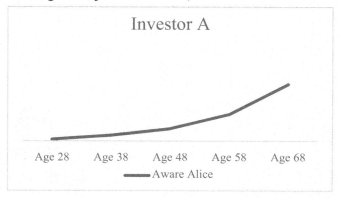

Investor A

Age 28   Age 38   Age 48   Age 58   Age 68
——— Aware Alice

Procrastinator Paul

Paul starts with the same salary at age 18, but he falls prey to the Risk of Procrastination. He doesn't invest in their twenties or even most of their thirties. At age thirty-eight, he makes some financial changes, and he begins to invest $1,200 per year from age 38 to 68, for a total of 30 years.

At age 48, he has $18,344 saved.

At age 58, with the additional $100 invested each month over the course of that decade, that investment has grown to more than $57,732.

At age 68, with the additional $100 invested each month over the course of another decade, that investment has grown to nearly $142,768.

So, by the time Procrastinator Paul is ready to retire at age 68, that investment has grown to nearly $143,000.

Procrastinator Paul actually invested for a longer amount of time than Aware Alice, adding to the account for thirty years instead of only ten. However, Procrastinator Paul started investing at a later season in life, so that money only had 30 years of compounding, while Aware Alice's account had 40 years of compounding. Even though Paul invested $36,100 over a lifetime – compared to Aware Alice's $12,000 over her lifetime, Procrastinator Paul retired with almost $250,000 less than Aware Alice.

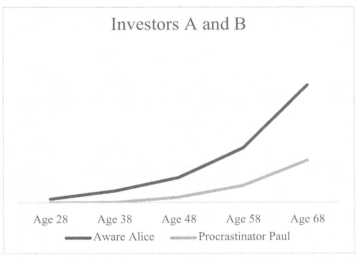

Keep-After-It Kate

Kate starts investing at age 18, setting aside $100 a month to invest $1,200 per year.

131

Invest Now

She keeps this pattern for ten years, and in that first decade of saving, her investment grows to $18,344. By sticking to the plan, things really paid off. *Watch this—*

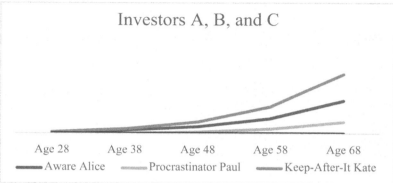

Kate kept after it, continuing to set aside $100 a month for all of her working years. While that original decade's worth of $12,000 compounded for forty years, Keep-After-It Kate continued to earn gains on her gains.

At age 28, with the additional 12k she saved in this decade, Kate's portfolio grew to more than $18,344

At age 38, with the additional 12k she saved in this decade, Kate's portfolio grew to $57,732.

At age 48, with the additional 12k she saved in this decade, Kate's portfolio grew to $142,768.

At age 58, with the additional 12k she saved in this decade, Kate's portfolio grew to $326,353.

And by the time Kate is ready to retire at age 68, her investments have grown to $722,700.

Ultimately, Keep-After-It Kate put about 59k into the account throughout her career, but with the power of compound interest, the strength of longevity, and the growing numbers of her continued savings, this original $59,000 grew to more than $722,000.

Traveler Tom

Tom starts investing at age 18, setting aside $100 a month to invest $1,200 per year. He too keeps this pattern for ten years, and his investment grew to $18,344 in that first decade of saving. But Traveler Tom has different goals  and seeks to travel the world. Traveler Tom utilizes his accrued interest as income for an epic vacation every ten years.

At age 28, his investments had grown to $18,344. Tom withdrew 10k for a vacation to Greece. The portfolio dipped to $8k.

At age 38, the investment had grown to over $36,142. Tom withdrew 12k for a vacation to New Zealand. The portfolio dipped to $24,142.

At age 48, that 24k has grown to more than $70,249. Tom withdrew 14k for a vacation to Thailand. The portfolio dipped to $56,249.

At age 58, that investment has grown to $143,269. Tom withdrew $18k for an African safari. The portfolio dipped to $125,269.

Invest Now

And by the time Tom is ready to retire at age 68, that portfolio has grown to $296,468.

Ultimately, Tom put about 59k into the account throughout their career, but they also withdrew 54k for a series of lifetime goals.

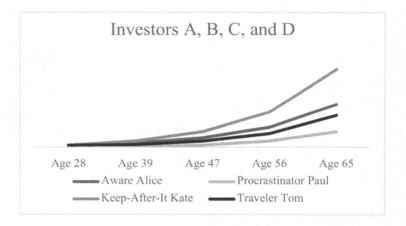

Is this case study of investors an example of compound interest? Or is this an example of why to start investing early? Or is this an example of letting your money grow without withdrawing your dividends?

Yes. It's all of these.

Each of these investors traveled a different route. The longer you have for your interest to compound, the more powerful it is. This is why it's important to get started saving now.

How did it work out for each one?

Aware Alice did well. She started early and let her money work hard with time in the market, and she's now enjoying her golden years the way she dreamed. Well done, Alice.

Procrastinator Paul ended up with dramatically less than Alice, despite contributing the same amount. Paul had to dig much deeper when he started saving money later in life, and his ending balance was a fraction of Alice's nest egg.

Keep-After-It Kate nailed it. She started young and kept on going. In the end, her balance was much higher than anyone else. Kate gets all the gold stars and trophies.

Traveler Tom set some real goals and spent his money the way he wanted to, but ultimately, he stole from his retirement by interrupting the investment process so many times. If Tom had established a vacation bucket, and if he had channeled money and dividends toward that bucket all along, he could have funded those vacations without interrupting his retirement fund.

Which one of these investors can you relate to? Whose path looks most like yours? If your path hasn't taken the upward trajectory you wish it had, remember: you can make changes today to get well on your way. You've picked up this book, and that's a good start.

CHAPTER TWELVE

Let Your Money Work for You
Enjoying Retirement

*"Two of the hardest things to do in life are to save when you
are young and spend when you are old. Learn balance in life.
Don't' be a spendthrift, but don't be a miser either."*
~ Mark Skousen (Editor of *Forecasts & Strategies* and
Author of *Maxims of Wall Street*)

Retirement looks different for each person, and your retirement
likely will not look like your parents' retirement. It's exciting to
see that retirees today are living longer, healthier lives – and I love
helping you plan for it.

Some people enjoy planning for the future. They set aside
savings with life goals in mind so they can live a life they have in
mind when they retire. Others want to live their lives as it unfolds,
and they intend to adjust to retirement when the time comes, living

on whatever the money situation turns out to be. Sometimes I meet with people who plan to work and save for another thirty years. Other times, I meet with people who have recently retired, and now they need to decide if it's possible. Sometimes they say, "I just retired. Tell me what to do next."

Sometimes people have saved every month, and some are worried they haven't saved enough. Some people choose to say, "This is what I need for retirement, and you need to show me what to save to get there." Other people say, "I'm going to save as best I can, I'll let you invest it, and when the time comes, I'll live on whatever that allows me to do."

These are not better or worse, but they are based on lifestyles and personalities. Your unique approach depends on how much structure you prefer. When people feel anxiety about their accounts or insecure with their level of savings, I prefer to help them look at it with new eyes. You always have a choice. Let's evaluate where you are. Let's see what this money can do for you.

Maybe you're looking forward to relaxing, no more bad days at work, no more battling the rush hour traffic to get home, no more of the daily grind. Perhaps you have some hobbies you're interested in pursuing, some activities that have been sitting in the margins of your life. Maybe you're a marathoner, and you're interested in completing Ironman Triathlons. Maybe you're ready to travel the world.

The concept of retirement can even differ within households. Throughout the years, I've seen a shift toward separate finances within one relationship, including some married couples with separate retirement plans. Career paths and investment goals are often personalized to individuals, rather than aligned as couples. More and more often, one person wants to travel more, while the other wants to settle in at home, so you'll see separate vacationing: Girls' Weekends. Guys' Fishing Trips. Sisters and Moms Getting Away. Guys golfing, fly fishing, and enjoying the country club. The world belongs to everyone now, in any way they choose to see it. We do things now that our grandparents could only imagine – or couldn't even imagine. Jet setting is a relatively new concept.

So, what do you have in mind? Where would you like to go? How fast do you want to get there? What do you have set aside, and what are you working toward?

Let yourself imagine what you want your retirement to look like – whether you're retiring in a year or in a few decades. How do you imagine your retirement? What ideas come to mind? Let yourself dream, and even write it down. Written goals become realities.

Retirement Anxiety

Perhaps the word retirement evokes a sense of concern if you're worried you haven't saved a certain amount of money by a certain age. Perhaps you're starting to fear that life stage – and the planning involved – because you haven't done what the experts say you should have done. Retirement can be a very stressful time, for sure. In fact, for many people, the few years before retirement are the most stressful years of an adult life, often the most stress they have encountered since having kids. In fact, retirement can be as stressful as getting married, losing your job, or having a close family member become ill.[41] Why is this life transition so nerve-wracking?

I believe it's because the choices are so many, and there is so much change at one time. Without a sense of direction, a person can feel paralyzed to take the next step. There can be great stress in knowing what to do with our days. When you have spent forty years going into the office, then a Monday morning without a plan can feel like the edge of a cliff.

People who are good savers are often scared to spend money. It's hard to imagine life without a paycheck. They wonder, How can I eat if I don't have a job? How can I pay my mortgage? How does one set a budget without income from a job?

Ultimately, they need to know how to break this down to a monthly budget. When they begin mapping it out in their mind, envisioning their retirement options, then they can begin to feel comfortable with the fact that the money will do its job.

"People will bring me their statement, and they'll say, "This may not be much to you, but it's all I have." First of all, it's not mine. It's yours. And it's worth everything to you. No matter how much it is, a retirement fund is a lot of money to the person holding the fund.

In this chapter, we will look at a variety of retirement questions and suggestions so you can craft a plan that works for you.

Your retirement doesn't have to be the most stressful season of your life. Entire books have been written on each of these topics, so I will share my insights on each, combined with my study, experiences, and personal expertise. Let's discuss some points of awareness that can make a difference. As you approach your retirement years, certain questions rise to the surface as most important to ask.

How Long Will Your Retirement Last?

Over the last century, life expectancy has gone up dramatically in the United States. In 1900, the average life expectancy was 49.2 years, and now the current life expectancy stretches into the late seventies. One out of three males and one out of two females in their fifties today will live to age 90. For a 65-year-old couple, that life expectancy goes up even more: there is a 50% chance that one of them will live to age 92. (CDC National Center for Health Statistics, 2018.)

When the current retirement age was agreed upon, in the late 1800s, that age was based – at least in part – on the fact that the average person didn't live as long. But with all of the advances in technology, research, science, and medicine, it's possible that today's retirees may live far longer than their ancestors.

How Long Will Retirement Last?

49.2 years

78.6 years

—Life Expectancy

How Much will Retirement Cost?

Some projections estimate that retirees will need to generate from 60-90% of their working income to pay for their retirement, but these projections are not always a realistic idea of what you might need. Instead, look at your current expenses, and decide which of those will remain after you retire. Be sure to include anyone who depends on your financial support, including children, grandchildren, or other dependents in your life.

For example, you likely will not have the expenses of a long commute from your working years, or the need to maintain a professional wardrobe. But there may be some details of your working lifestyle that you'd like to maintain, such as lawncare, salons or spas, and pet care. If you enjoy those services before your retirement, you may want to enjoy them in your retirement as well. Remember, even though you enter a new phase of life, you are the same person with the same interests, hobbies, and joy for life. Make a realistic assessment of what is important to you, even if it may not be important to someone else.

Increasing healthcare costs are a concern for most retirees. You may no longer be covered by your former employer's healthcare, and you are probably tasked with purchasing insurance on your own. This brings up the many questions about the benefits and limitations of Medicare. For many, the best course may be to appropriately budget for healthcare costs in retirement.

Naturally, there are some costs we can foresee and control, and others we cannot. One factor we can expect is the effect of inflation, the general increase in the prices of goods and services. We have talked about how a dollar buys less as its value decreases over time – remember, we said inflation is like diluting a perfect cup of coffee with more water. Consider the long-term trends in consumer prices in order to best estimate how much money you may expect to need.

Once you have estimated the income you may need, you can estimate the cost of the retirement you envision.

In the back of this book, you'll find some bonus material that includes a retirement budget worksheet. My team designed this to give you a starting point for to plan your retirement income

Generating Your Retirement Income

What sources of income (your buckets) do you anticipate you will have? Let's take a look at what you can expect. Traditionally, retirement funding has been viewed as a "three-legged stool", implying a balance between Social Security, retirement plans, and any other savings and investments. The most common income-generating investments are individual bonds, income-oriented mutual funds, and fixed annuities. For peace of mind, you will want to consider a long-term approach for each of these streams of income, in hopes that they will not run dry too soon.

So, let's say Investor Evan has invested in the following buckets: a brokerage account, a 401(k), an IRA, and he's planning to receive Social Security benefits. Each one accounts for 20% of his retirement plan. Instead of draining his brokerage account first to fund his retirement, we'll prorate the payments so that each one makes up 20% of his monthly retirement income. Rather than draw-

How Will You Pay for Retirement?

Expected Sources, according to Retirees

Actual Sources, according to Retirees

■ Employer Sponsored Plan ■ Social Security ■ Work   ■ Employer Sponsored Plan ■ Social Security ■ Work

ing all of his monthly income from one account, he'll take a little bit from five different places. This way, none of the buckets should ever run dry.

At the beginning of this book, we talked about the psychology of investing. One of the biggest factors of success is the *feeling* that things are under control. We have discovered that this is a way to mitigate the fears of retirement: to keep all the buckets intact.

Invest Now

There is an old set of rules in retirement planning, and one was this: if you have a brokerage account and you have an IRA, you spend down the brokerage account first, and then you spend the IRA. The idea behind that is that the IRA is still growing, tax deferred. It made sense.

But here's one thing I've learned over the years: if someone has two big accounts and they spend down one of them – even as a strategy, they start to freak out because one of their accounts is gone. We needed a new way to generate income without letting any single bucket run dry.

We have learned that a sensible goal – and a far less emotional approach – is to keep all the buckets maintained through retirement. How do we keep them all afloat? By prorating the distributions from all accounts. In other words, keep all the buckets intact.

Social Security

Social Security is a safety net of sorts, basically designed to keep you from living on the street in your later years. It is not designed to replace your full income, and it doesn't make for a comfortable retirement for most people. Yes, plan for Social Security, but plan for it to be just one of your buckets.

Lean in close, because this is important: ***Social Security is not a savings plan***. All the money you pay into the system will not be waiting for you later, like a 401(k). It's a pay-as-you-go system, so the money you pay as you're working is actually paying for people who are living their retirement now. This may seem unfair, for your paycheck to fund someone else's golden years, but fear not: your retirement income will be paid by people in the workforce of the future. (Hopefully.)

Social Security has faced a major challenge in the last few years, as the number of people who are expected to depend on these benefits has increased, while the number of people paying into the system has decreased. That gap is expected to widen, as Social Security is paying out more than it takes in.

Currently, Social Security is designed to replace 40% of income for most Americans, and the amount you receive is based on your 35 highest years of earning income. However, as these funds are depleted, the benefits may need to be adjusted and reduced. Social Security may not always be able to provide enough for anyone's sole source of retirement income.

To see how much your estimated payout will be, you can visit the Social Security Administration's website, at www.ssa.gov/myaccount.

When Should You Take Social Security?

The full retirement age is 65, but the Social Security program allows you to start receiving benefits early as age 62 or to delay your benefits all the way until the age of 70. What is the best timing, and why?

Monthly payments vary quite a bit, depending on when you start

Today's average life expectancy is 77 years: 74 for men, and 79 for women.

145

Invest Now

receiving the benefits. The Social Security Administration has
based the math on a fairly reliable formula: if a person lives to the
average life expectancy, that person will receive roughly the same
amount in lifetime benefits, no matter when they start receiving
them. The actual math is not quite that simple and straightforward,
but the principle still holds, based on the key phrase: "if a person
lives to average life expectancy."

When Social Security was established, very few people lived
long enough to collect the benefits for more than a few years.
Today's average life expectancy is 77 years: an average based on
an expectancy rate of 74 for men, and 79 for women.[42]

Consider this: in today's longevity, a healthy man at age 65
has a 50% chance of living beyond age 85, and a healthy woman
at age 65 has that same chance of living beyond age 88. Twenty-
five percent of those same seniors have a chance of living beyond
the age of 92 for men (94 for women). For a healthy couple, both
65, there is a 50% chance one will live beyond the age of 92, and a
25% chance one will live beyond the age of 97.[43]

If a person lives longer than the average life expectancy
(which is happening more and more and more), they will
accumulate more from Social Security over the course of a
lifetime.

If you begin receiving Social Security benefits at an earlier
age, the monthly check will be smaller. The longer you wait to
begin, the larger each monthly check will be. The person who
started to receive benefits at age 62 would receive $652,320 by the

age of 85, while another person who started to receive benefits at age 70 would receive $727,680 by the age of 85.[2]

There is no single right answer to the question of when to start benefits, as the decision is based on many factors, including family considerations, economic assets, and personal preferences.

The Bull Market and the Bear Market Affect Retirement

The timing of your retirement can affect your retirement living, depending on whether you retire during a Bull Market or a Bear Market. If a couple retires in a Bull Market, and their investments are doing well due to a rise in the market, then their account may continue to grow despite withdrawals. If a couple retires during a turbulent season in the economy, if that same couple withdrew the same amount of money, the strategy could have detrimental effects on their balance and their entire retirement. The first few years of withdrawals will make a great difference in the long-term trajectory of the retirement plan.

Revisiting Your Asset Allocation

As we have mentioned, asset allocation is one of the most important factors in a sound investment plan, and this is even more true during retirement. There is a higher sense of urgency to manage investment risk. Asset allocation does not guarantee

---

[2] This assumes the maximum retirement benefit of $3,011 at age 66, and it does not include a cost-of-living adjustment.

147

against investment loss, but rebalancing is an ongoing process. You are wise to understand which of your assets are performing best, and plan accordingly for your stocks, bonds, and cash alternatives. **Be sure that your portfolio reflects your intent as well as your risk tolerance.**

How Much of My Portfolio Can I Take Out?

This is a very important question as you begin your retirement. After all, your growth plan has now become an income plan. Withdraw too quickly, and your money could indeed be

Four Percent Rule:

You can withdraw 4% of your savings each year, while the rest of your investments continue to grow.

gone too soon. Spend too slowly, and you might deprive yourself of some of life's pleasures. To calculate your spending, become familiar with the **Four Percent Rule.**

Generally speaking, the four percent rule enables you to withdraw 4% of your savings each year while the rest of your investments continue to grow. So, if you have $1 million in your retirement account, you can withdraw $40,000 the first year, then another four percent the following year, for at least thirty years.

Wall Street will tell you that you should never take out more than 4% of your money, but reality says you can take out more. Again, that advice is in their best interests, not yours. They're trying to keep your money in the market because the more assets they have, the more money they make.

Yes, you can take out more, but the 4% rule is a stable one to guide your planning, especially as you begin your retirement. The strategies and patterns you put into place in first year or two can make or break your retirement. If you start a withdrawal scenario that's too aggressive, and if the market takes a severe downturn and you cannot adjust your plans, then your retirement could be severely impacted. If you have flexibility to take out less, then you have room to recover.

The 4% rule provides a framework for a solid start that your portfolio can maintain.

There is an ever-shifting balance with your buckets. You never want to stress your buckets, to try to create a stronger stream of income than the source can provide. But also, the goal is not to have as much money in the buckets as you can when you die. The goal is to live your life while you're here, while it's yours to live.

The Truth of Traveling

Since Americans are living much longer than they used to, this longevity adds a layer of complexity to retirement planning – and especially to the travel plans. If you retire at 65, you likely still have twenty years in front of you—or sometimes even more. So, now that you're stepping into retirement, there's a question to ask: How long will you live?

Invest Now

It sounds morbid and even fatalistic, but it's a key element to retirement planning. In a practical sense, let's be honest about this. People who expect to live into their nineties will plan and spend differently than someone likely to die younger. Some people know that their genetic makeup doesn't project a long lifetime, so they spend differently than someone with a different family history.

Here's the truth of traveling: Most people are done with their life's biggest adventures by the time they are eighty years old. That doesn't mean life is over, it doesn't mean they don't get to have fun, and it doesn't mean they're not contributing to society and enjoying the most of every day. What it means, genuinely, is they are done with their physically- and mentally-taxing traveling. They're likely to stay closer to home, inside the United States, and making plans on a smaller scale. There are some exceptions, but for the most part, people are done traveling the world by the time they're in their eighties—whether they want to be or not.

When people work until they're 75, they are lucky to get five years of strenuous travel before they need to stay closer to home. If they have been excessively coached to "save, save, save" for the years to come, they miss out on their most adventurous seasons - in their sixties and seventies, if not sooner. It's like a scale. If you want to go see Europe or Africa, you need to do that right away. If you want to go see the Grand Canyon, you can do that anytime down the road.

In my years as an advisor, I've seen people who are literally scared to spend the money they've saved. Truly, spending requires a whole new way of thinking. Learn how to spend the appropriate amount of your assets so you can enjoy the fourth quarter of their life. The sooner that you can get comfortable with that concept, the better retirement you will have.

There are countless ways to maximize your travel opportunities in retirement, to make your money go as far as it can go – literally and figuratively! Some airlines and hotels have dining rewards programs so you can accumulate points and eat for less. Airline credit cards are great ways to cut the cost of air travel, assuming you pay the balance every month. You can utilize those cards for your everyday needs, and those dollars add up to become miles in the air. Choose your next credit card by deciding where and when you want to travel.[44]

Travel where you want to go and do the activities you want to do—whatever they are, while you are able. Time is ticking, and your money is yours to enjoy while you can.

Make Peace with Your Money

Eric Thurman wrote a book called *Thrive in Retirement: Simple Secrets for Being Happy for the Rest of Your Life.* Thurman's book is filled with insights for maximizing these decades of your life, focusing on five core categories: mind, body, relationships, finances, and soul. His book takes the mystery out of aging, and I highly recommend it to you – whether you've just retired, you're about to retire, or just trying to wrap your mind around the retirement lifestyle.

Thurman's chapter on finances offers a refreshing perspective: how you think about your money will mightily affect your happiness. Even people who are financially quite secure can get into the habit of living in a state of worry over their finances. One study showed that about one-half of millionaires with net worth of up to $5 million felt insecure, fearing they could lose it all.[45]

He believes that the three principles of happiness are purpose, pleasure, and peace. So, you will not be happy unless you are at peace with your finances, find a purpose for your life that is separate from your money, and derive pleasure from other sources than having or spending money.

How do you make peace with your money? Eric Thurman gives the following guidelines:

Clarify Your Dreams. He quotes Dr. Bill Hall, a man who knows quite a bit about money. Dr. Hall has been a business professor at two universities, a CFO of a large company, and he finished his own retirement years an executive coach to CEOs. Dr. Hall says this small assignment helps people identify what they truly want in their future: "Write down your thoughts about what would be a perfect day for you five years from now."[46] He has one rule, and that is that a great vacation or a new car don't count as dreams for this assignment, since nobody can buy a car every day or travel all the time. So, what is it that sounds like a perfect day for you, five or ten years from now? Write it down. Make that your goal.

Know Your Finish Lines. He quotes David Wills, who said, "I encourage people to have clear finish lines, an annual finish line, and a lifetime finish line." Finish lines are a way to think about budgets and estate planning. Rather than worrying about how much money you have or don't have, consider a realistic goal for how you'd like to end the year financially, as well as what you want to give to others when you die. People often suffer from not knowing how much they have or how much is enough, and these finish lines can set targets of satisfaction.

Protect Your Family. He's not talking here about self-defense, insurance, or gun safety. He's talking about the destruction of family conflict, which I've seen firsthand. People don't like to think about dying, so they're often unprepared for the end of life. Without a plan, they leave their family to resolve their affairs—and often drown in conflict with one another. Prepare your affairs so your family will have nothing to fight over, not a mess to untangle.

Give to Others. Some people want to give it all to their kids, and others have an organization, school, or institution they would like to endow with a gift. Everyone has a different outlook, but there tends to be a clear connection between generosity and happiness. Thurman again quoted Dr. David Wills, who said, "When I see people get older and also get less happy, I can almost guarantee that as they've gotten older, they've become less generous."[47]

Your gifts to others do not have to be money you leave behind when you're gone. You have many assets to give, and finances may be a good place to begin, but consider other options as well. Take a vacation with your family and give them tangible memories. Give your time, skills, and wisdom. These are generous gifts as well, and they can be the key to your greatest joys in this season of life.

CHAPTER THIRTEEN

Q & A
Real-Life Questions from Real, Live People

"An investment in knowledge pays the best interest."
~ Ben Franklin

What are the most common mistakes people make?

There are many common mistakes people make in their planning for retirement, and these issues have implications that deeply affect their financial future.

• **Speculating instead of Investing.** People often get distracted by the fast moves of speculating, moving their money around to try to beat the market or make a quick buck. Investing is a long-term choice in a company you believe in. You'll own a slice of the companies you invest in, so choose companies with strong leadership and a positive track record of success. This applies whether you're buying an individual company, or bundles of stocks through mutual funds and ETFs. Either way, invest your money and stay the course.

- **Becoming too Conservative.** Yes, careful, intentional choices are a good thing, but there are ways that you can deprive or even rob yourself—of money and of the lifestyle you want to enjoy. If you keep your money only in savings, CDs, and money markets, the purchasing power of your dollars will decrease as inflation grows. You'll find yourself with less money in the end. If you get so good at saving that you never learn how to spend the money you've saved, you'll miss out on the whole point of the plan. Don't get so conversative that you miss out on the good things.

- **Underestimating Tax Rates.** People often imagine that their tax rates will be lower than they planned, and that is rarely the case. The taxman will get his share, which is why 401(k), IRA, and Roth accounts are important to consider. Plan accordingly, and don't be surprised by the money you'll owe.

- **Not Enough Buckets.** Sometimes people make the mistake of believing their timeline is too short for them to diversity effectively. Let me tell you: diversification across asset classes can be the winning strategy for any timeline.

- **Confusing Life Insurance as an Investment.** A life insurance policy is not a savings account, and while there are many types of insurance, they generally will not pay out as investments. Keep them separate from your investment buckets.

- **Too Much Noise.** People can become distracted by the chatter of talking heads and the swinging pendulum of headlines. Chart your course, and then stay in your lane.
- **Waiting to Begin.** Get started today. You'll always be thankful you did.

Should I use a 401(k) or an IRA to save for retirement? Traditional account, or Roth type?

This is a good question, and there are many factors that determine the best solution. First of all, it depends on your age. The younger you are, the more likely you should utilize the Roth IRA. The longer that your investment can grow tax free—and later withdrawn tax free—the better off you will be.

With an IRA, nobody matches your contribution, and there is a $6500 limit per year. So, if your employer has a company match for the 401(k), this should be your first go-to. If there's a match from your employer, it's like getting a raise. People often make the mistake of only contributing up to the match, but this is the bare minimum. You can add more than that. Shoot for a goal of 10-15% of income to go to into some sort of savings on a regular and consistent basis.

Are there any retirement issues that are unique to women?

Each woman is unique in her own right, and each one will have her own personal experiences with work, finances, and retirement. Historically, we have seen women as a collective face some specific issues as they face retirement, and those deserve to be addressed in a way that empowers women.

Based on median statistics, women tend to live longer, but they have fewer years of earned income, and they've often not invested until later in life. Women are usually the ones carrying the physical, emotional, and financial load of caring for both children and elderly parents. And because women tend to live longer, they are more statistically inclined to die single, divorced, or widowed.

Women can mitigate their experiences by keeping a close eye on the following:

- Have access to all of your household's income, expenses, assets, and liabilities, including online information, accounts, loans, credit cards, and insurance policies.

- Know where all your investment accounts are and familiarize yourself with the asset allocation plan.

- Know where to locate key documents.

- Meet all of your family's advisors, including an estate attorney, accountant, insurance agent, and financial advisor. Be sure to know their names and be sure they know yours.

- Understand clearly how much you will need to have saved to maintain your standard of living in retirement. Find out how much you can comfortably afford to spend without running out of money.

- With the expectation of living longer, make sure to plan on covering the care you may need in your later years.

What are some resources, links, websites that help me along my investing journey?

Marketwatch.com

CNBC.com

Kiplinger

MotleyFool

Investor.gov

Wall Street Journal

Investment advisors' updates and websites, including my company, Cherry Creek Investment Advisors, at cherrycreekinvestmentadvisors.com. If you go to our website, you can add yourself to our free weekly market update.

Remember to avoid the noisemakers. Don't get inundated or flooded with information, because too much information can cause panic and fear.

Avoid information overload. Pay attention only to the things you can control. You have no control other than getting started, putting your money to work, managing your risk, and turning off the noise.

How should an investor choose a financial advisor, and what point is one necessary?

This is different for everyone. Even if you feel fully capable of handling these decisions on your own, it's also absolutely okay to decide you don't want to do it. Someone who is investing only $100 a month may still want an advisor to get them started in the process. Someone else may have built up their portfolios, and they don't need an advisor until it becomes too complex to handle. There are people with millions of dollars who can manage it themselves, and there are some with $500 who choose to move out of the driver's seat and let someone else handle it.

The best advantage of an advisor is their ability to take the emotionality out of investing. An experienced advisor—one with a high level of experience and education—will be wise to the cycles of the market, and they will keep you from overreacting to stressful financial situations. When stocks are falling and fear is rising, you could make a costly mistake. This is where a financial advisor is worth every penny.

A few items to keep in mind as you choose the right financial advisor for you:

• Look for fee-based payments. Your advisor should receive no commissions.

• You need an independent advisor who is only getting paid by their clients, not receiving kickbacks from pushy companies selling their products. Never hire an advisor who sells a product to you to make their living.

• Make a list of candidates. Run a background check and check their credentials.

• Always interview your advisor, and plan on more than a 30-second call on the phone. Ask how long they've been in the business. Ask about their typical clients, to see if you match their specialty and focus. Ask them to clarify their fees and ask for three client references.

- Is this someone you're comfortable with? If not, keep looking. Every advisor has clients who reflect their personality, and if it's not a match, then it won't ever be a good fit.
- If you're going to take the time to hire an advisor: Listen to them. Don't argue with them. You hired an expert, so let them utilize their expertise.

If I'm in my first job, how do I even begin to invest? What advice to you give to a young person with their first real job income?

How old are they? Is it a part time job in high school, or is it their first job moving forward in their career? If it's a teenager, do a Roth. Parents can match it.

If it's a career job with a 401(k), get started with your employer. Get the maximum amount you can.

In most cases, you should start with the Roth version instead of the regular version. A lot of 401(k) plans come with a website, a lot of Q and A, maybe even a consultant to answer your questions. Take advantage of that. Get an education wherever you can, especially for free.

How much money do I need?

Invest Now

This is not a one-size-fits-all answer. It depends on many factors, including:

General advice and conventional wisdom say that most retirees will need 70-80% of their pre-retirement income to live comfortably in their later years.

This number is changing as retirement costs are shifted or eliminated. For example, you may not have the expenses you had in your working years, including commuting, business lunches, professional wardrobe, business trips, and memberships to organizations. On the flip side, retirement expenses also shift with healthcare, travel plans, and lifestyle.

Depending on your timing and your goals, it might be too late to accumulate as much as you would like, and you may need to adjust to making do with what you have. This is not a bad thing, and remember, you always have choices.

Will I run out of money?

If you have been disciplined enough to save your money for retirement, you need to also be disciplined enough to take it out intentionally and carefully. Your success depends on as little debt as possible. Live within your means and enjoy a retirement that matches your financial reality.

Should I buy an annuity?

162

No. I mean, they work for some people. But you probably should not.

Here's how an annuity works: you give an insurance company your money, then they promise to pay you an income stream for an established number of years, hopefully the rest of your life. In some annuities, if you die before you've received your money back, your family will not receive the money you paid. Sometimes family members can receive cash back or even continued monthly income, but the annuity companies will charge you even more for that option.

Essentially, you give them your money, they invest it, and they trickle it back to you in small amounts – or with steep penalties. Annuities pay extremely high commission, so somebody else is making quite a profit on your money, and they're betting you die before you can get it back. This is not a system with your best interests in mind.

Generally, annuities have surrender fees that are highest if you take out the money in advance. Withdrawals and income payments are taxed as ordinary income, and annuities are not guaranteed by the FDIC or any other government agency.

Annuities work for some people, but not most. If you're considering an annuity, do a comparison to learn how much income and total return you'd likely earn if you invested that same amount in the stock market.

Can I Borrow from my 401(k)?

Invest Now

It's a fair question, given the options. In 2020, the average household with credit card debt had a balance of $7,149 which equates to an annual interest of $1,155. With the average credit card annual percentage rate sitting at 16.43%, this is an expensive way to fund spending.[48] So, does it make sense to borrow from my 401(k) to pay off debt or to make a major purchase?

There are some benefits to borrowing from your 401(k):

• No Credit Check. If you have a low credit score or trouble getting credit, then you'll be glad to know that borrowing from a 401(k) requires no credit check. As long as your 401(k) permits loans, you should be able to borrow.

• Convenient. Borrowing from your 401(k) usually requires minimal paperwork, and it is quicker than the alternative.

• Competitive Interest Rates. The rate you pay depends upon the terms your 401(k) sets out, but the rate is typically lower than the rate you will pay on personal loans or through a credit card. Plus, the interest you pay will be to yourself, rather than to a finance company.

There are some disadvantages as well:

• Most people who take loans from their 401(k) also stop contributing to that account. So, you'll lose the money you've borrowed, and you'll also lose the potential earnings and any matching contributions.

• Risk of Job Loss. If you decide to switch jobs or if you get laid off, your 401(k) loan becomes immediately due. If you do not have the cash to pay the balance, it will have tax consequences. A

164

401(k) loan not paid is deemed a distribution, subject to income taxes and a 10% penalty tax if you are under the age of 59½.

- Red Flag Alert. If you need to borrow from your retirement savings to fund your current expenditures, this could be a red flag indicating overspending. You may save money by paying off your high-interest credit-card balances, but if these balances run up again, you may have done yourself more harm.

Most financial experts caution against borrowing from your 401(k), but they also concede that a loan may be a more appropriate alternative to an outright distribution, if the funds are absolutely needed.

What can I do if I'm nearing retirement, but I don't have a plan?

You may not have a plan, but that doesn't mean you don't have any money. Take inventory of what you do have: your assets, and then take stock of your expenses, debts, and ongoing bills. With this information, you can begin to put a plan together. If you're near retirement without a plan, I recommend professional help. Why? Because a plan probably will not create itself.

The first thing they will ask you is what you have. Insurance, annuities, savings, investments, etc. Debts, mortgage, home value, car debt, credit card debt, personal loans, student loans, etc. From there, you can begin to put together a picture.

If you don't have a plan, that doesn't mean you're in trouble. But now is the time to make a plan. The older you are, the more you want to save, to make up for lost time. Sometimes people take on a second job for a year or two to beef up their savings. Saving anything today is better than saving nothing tomorrow. Put the most in there that you can. Fill those buckets. Get started.

It's never too late to begin. You'll always be glad you did.

I don't feel like I have enough money to retire comfortably in the United States. Can people retire overseas?

We are seeing this more and more often. People are moving to other countries - Costa Rica and Mexico are two destinations at the top of the list, and there are many others throughout the world. Every country has a different cost of living and a different economy. Quite often you can find communities of likeminded retirees who have all moved to these communities for the same reasons. So yes, it is easily done.

Are Reverse Mortgages a good idea?

The weightiest factor of a good retirement—more than how much money you've saved—is whether you have a mortgage to pay. Without a mortgage payment, retirees can live on a smaller budget and with far fewer expenses. If you own a home but you have not paid off your mortgage, you may not realize it, but there is good news tucked in there. Your house is another bucket for your finances.

For those who have not paid off their mortgage, **there's a tool called a reverse mortgage**. This can become a lifeline for seniors who are running out of money or who have had a rough start to retirement. The reverse mortgage can be a parachute bucket of last resort.

When you purchase a home and take out a mortgage, you borrow money, interest accrues every month, and you make monthly payments. A reverse mortgage is like that, only in reverse. You already own the house, the bank gives you the money up front, interest accrues every month, and the loan isn't paid back until you die or move out of the house. If you die, you never pay back the loan—your estate does. And your estate won't have to pay more than the value of the house.

Reverse mortgages were once considered the devil's business, as people who were desperate for cash got swindled with complicated transactions and high fees. It is a more common tool now, but you still want to make sure you understand exactly what you'll receive and what will be owed. Don't skip this step of the research.

Frankly, a reverse mortgage may be the bucket that is the difference between a boring retirement and fun retirement.

What about Medicare?

Medicare is the national health insurance program for people over the age of 65, and there are countless books, websites, and representatives who are experts in this topic. It's a complicated situation, but let's narrow it down to this: if you're appalled by the cost of insurance at your age, imagine how it shifts as you get older... or much older. For most people, the cost would be far out of reach. Medicare is complicated, but necessary.

It's easy to feel overwhelmed by the many layers and facets of Medicare, so let's look at the four major coverage options and some of their significant qualities.

Part A includes Hospital Coverage. This is the portion that pays hospital costs, home care, hospital care, and the first one hundred days of skilled nursing care. You likely paid for this during your working years, contributing through your payroll taxes, so you probably will not have a premium to pay for this level of care. The numbers shift a bit every year, regarding how much you have to pay for a hospital stay, how much Medicare will pay for how long, and at what point you will be responsible for the full cost of any additional days in the hospital.

Part B includes Medical Coverage. This portion covers outpatient health care visits, including doctor visits, outpatient surgeries, diagnostic testing, durable medical equipment, and any ambulance services. Part B is not free, and you'll pay premiums each month, depending on your income. You'll have a deductible for each year, and once it is met, you'll likely owe 20% for the cost of services.

Part C is known as the Medicare Advantage. These consist of private plans that bundle the benefits of Parts A and B, for only the cost of the standard Part B premium.

Part D includes Prescription Drug Coverage. These prescription drug plans are available to everyone who has

Medicare, as Medicare provides at least a standard level of prescription drug coverage. For additional coverage with a monthly premium, you can purchase a stand-alone plan or a bundle as part of Part C (Medicare Advantage) plans.

Medicare coverage begins when you turn 65, and you can enroll between three months before and three months after you turn 65. The best thing you can do is to sign up on time, so you do not encounter periods of time when you don't have coverage. Signing up late will raise your monthly premiums and costs for prescription medications, you'll likely end up paying more, and you may face premium penalties that can last for your entire lifetime.

Revisit your choices every year. Annually, Medicare has open enrollment from October 15 through December 7. This is your time to review your coverage and decide whether it still suits your needs and priorities. You'll want to determine if you still have the best choices of prescription coverage, given the drugs you take, since insurance carriers change their preferred provider pharmacies and prices each year. Insurance companies may be able to charge higher premiums, or they can deny coverage entirely. To avoid gaps, apply before your current coverage has ended.

So, mark your calendar, and get your name on Uncle Sam's list.

As a longtime client, you have talked a lot about buckets over the years. Why are these buckets so important?

169

Think of buckets as choices. We all want more choices. The more buckets you have for your money to grow, the more options and choices you have as avenues for your income.

Where do I get started? Who holds my investment accounts?

We have more answers to this question than any other time in history. Online, traditional, new competitors, IIP, personal help, completely online—there are more choices than ever, and finding help is now easier than ever before. And it used to be that people would only talk to you if you had a half million dollars – that's no longer true. Anyone can begin with any amount of money. Start with local investment advisors, banks, credit unions, and the 401(k) plan at your workplace.

I often hear maxims on Wall Street, like Sell in May and Go Away. Should I pay attention to these?

No. The media has created them to be headlines and sound bites. There are hundreds of these, each one has a little bit of truth, but you shouldn't base your investment plans on these. Keep the long-term view in mind.

What are short sellers?

There are people who make money when the market goes down. While most investors hope the market goes up, there are some investors, called **short sellers,** who make money when the market goes down. Short selling is a risky proposition, as it can backfire with unlimited loss, and the short sellers don't want that to happen to them. So, they are influencing the financial media, adding to the confusion and drama, and predicting doom and gloom for the market and companies.

Short sellers are not bad guys, and short selling does have some positive attributes for the overall market. I only bring it up here as an example of how Wall Street doesn't always have your back. If you're investing for the first time, and you come across one of these preachers of gloom and doom forecasting, you'd find it very unsettling. And yet, this happens every day, in newsletters, the financial channels, and the web.

What are your thoughts on investing in Precious Metals and Gold?

Gold has been one of the most popular commodities in the history of the world. It has been valued and highly sought after as far back as 4000 BC, and you have probably seen photos of ancient Egypt's golden treasures. In fact, there is not an era or major culture where gold has not been highly sought and seen as having a high value. From ancient Egypt to the Aztecs, China's many dynasties, the ancient Greek and Roman cultures all placed a high value on gold and it symbolized power and wealth.

Today, gold is seen as a hedge against inflation and a safe harbor during risky times. Most recently, gold prices have skyrocketed during Russia's invasion of Ukraine. In the month prior to and including the first few days of the invasion gold is up over 7 percent. Over the long-run, gold is seen as a harbor of value.

For instance, if you looked at the prices of a fine men's suit in the early 1900's the cost of that suit would have been approximately 1 ounce of gold. Today, despite 100 years of inflation, if you went to buy a man's fine man's suite it would cost approximately the same as an ounce of gold. While there are short periods of time where this may not be the case, due to spiking prices of gold or shrinking prices of suits, this ratio is a good comparison that stands the test of time.

Gold can be purchased physically, via U.S. minted gold coins, or privately minted gold bars or rounds, bullion coins. It can also be purchased via ETFs. Both have their advantages and disadvantages.

If you choose to take physical delivery of your gold, I suggest U.S. minted gold eagles as the best vehicle in which to do that. These coins have been available since 1986, and they are available in sizes ranging from 1/10 of an ounce to one full ounce in size. They are relatively portable and recognized throughout the world. They are liquid, as almost every town in America has coin dealer or shop nearby. Other countries carry similar coins, like the Canadian Maple Leaf. Of course, since gold bars and coins are a physical commodity, you need to make sure you have a safe place to store them.

Gold ETFs trade like stocks, but they are either backed by physical gold or tied to gold via the futures market. They are super liquid and can be bought and sold easily to take advantage of short-term price swings. Clearly, you don't have a storage problem with ETFs—but you also don't have the power of gold in your hand either.

What should I know about Cryptocurrency? Is it a real thing, and is it here to stay?

Just like gold is one of the oldest commodities in the world, cryptocurrency is one of the newest. Cryptocurrency is digital money that only exists online. It is exchanged virtually and secured against hackers. Cryptocurrency refers to the entire universe of technologies that involves blockchains, the shared databases that store information in a cryptographically safe way. The information is maintained on a network of computers all over the world.

The New York Times says Crypto may be "the single fastest way to freshen your cultural awareness and decipher the beliefs and actions of today's young people."[49] It's up and coming, and it's important to pay attention to, as it's going to be a transformative force in our society in the years to come. If we don't pay attention to it, if we give it a skeptical, passing glance, then it may become a destructive force. Let's not allow that to happen to us.

How do I know if I'm putting my money into a good investment? How do you know if you've been given good advice?

This is a good question with a complicated answer. First, make sure your advisor is not selling a product. They should receive no commission or kickback from another company. Specifically stay away from insurance products – these are not investments. You don't want to invest in something that someone else is making an incentive on.

Your advisor should not benefit from loads or commissions. You want low costs, low internal fees, and liquidity. Don't get caught in the latest mouse trap. Invest in things that have been around for a long time.

Ask yourself, *Are you comfortable with what they're telling you?* Trust your instincts and back away from something that doesn't feel right. Today's markets are no place for dabblers without time, patience, discipline, and diligence required to do a proper job.

There are no investments you can buy and then forget about. The pace of change is too great for investors to be complacent, so you need to aggressively monitor your investments, or pay someone skilled to do it for you.

In Conclusion:

One of the key differences between successful long-term investors and those who are not, is this: successful investors learn from their own mistakes and commit to never making the same mistake twice. Don't deceive yourself with these words: "This time it's different." They are the costliest words in the history of investing, and the best thing you can do is pause, take a step back, and review the actions that led to this loss. Determine where you went astray and take steps to avoid the same mistake in the future. Let that be the variable that's different: your choices. In today's world of high-tech investing, major financial decisions are only a click away, and investors pay a high price for short-term thinking. Don't let that happen to you.

Many common investing mistakes can be traced back to emotional decision making. Whenever you make financial or investment decisions, you will confront the competing challenges of two beasts: fear and greed. Fear can cause you to run for the exits when markets decline, or your portfolio takes losses. Greed can encourage you to chase fads and take on too much risk in the pursuit of a big score. By recognizing your emotional triggers and engaging instead with your rational mind, you can overcome impulses, cultivate discipline, and stay the course.

Working with a financial planner can help avoid emotional decisions and many other pitfalls. It is our job to remain focused on the long-term strategy, and to act as a voice of reason when emotions run high. Professional representatives can be invaluable in their ability to answer questions, provide reassurance, and keep financial strategies on track, even in the face of volatile conditions.

Long-term investing success requires discipline, time, and skill. While it's impossible to predict future returns or market movements, it is possible to develop strategies that mitigate risk and place you in the best position to achieve reasonable returns. No strategy is perfect, but my experience has shown that the principles in this book can guide you to achieve financial success over the long-term.

In the opening pages of this book, we talked about flight attendants and the announcements they give to guide us on our journey. With that in mind, let's circle back and bring this flight to a close. Please hear the following in the voice of your favorite flight attendant speaking into the microphone as your plane lands.

Ladies and Gentlemen, this is Sean Castle welcoming you to this new understanding of investing, where the current temperature is inviting. Please check around you for any personal belongings you'd like to protect with your next egg. I encourage you to please use caution as you open new accounts, as market trends shift during the journey. At this time, you may use your cellular devices if you wish, but I do recommend you turn off notifications to all market ups and downs. These will only cause turbulence in your spirit and your soul. If you require investment assistance, one of our financial planners will be pleased to assist you.

On behalf of your financial future, I'd like to thank you for joining us on this trip. We look forward to seeing you in the near future.

Turn off the noise and get started now.

Retirement Budget Planner

Many retirees want to know how much income they will need in order to live comfortably in their retirement. My team has designed this worksheet to give you a starting point for planning for your retirement income.

Start with your current bills and spending habits, filling in each category of the budget worksheet. Use your bank statements, credit card bills, and financial account statements to record your spending in each area.

Using your current spending as a guide, estimate how much you will spend in each category in retirement. Remember that most retirees spend close to their pre-retirement levels in most areas, except in the categories of food, transportation, clothing, and other job-related expenses. Medical expenses may go up as you transition away from employer-sponsored health insurance, and as you begin planning for long-term medical needs.

Think about major purchases you might like to make, including remodeling your kitchen, buying a new car, or upgrading household appliances. Think about what's on your bucket list, like milestone vacations or charitable gifts.

Profiling your retirement expenses is an important first step in planning for a comfortable retirement, but it is only the beginning. Your spending patterns will change over time with inflation, market returns, and your changing needs—but this is a great first step.

Housing	Current	In retirement
Mortgage/Rent		
Electricity		
Gas/Oil		
Water/Sewer/Trash		
Phone		
Cable & Internet		
Appliances & Furniture		
Maintenance & Improvements		
Lawn & Garden Care		
Household Supplies		
Property Tax & Insurance		
Total Housing		

Daily Living	Current	In retirement
Groceries		
Beverages & Alcohol		
Personal Products		
Clothing		
Dry Cleaning		

Salon & Barber Visits		
Total Daily Living		

Health and Medical	Current	In retirement
Medical and Dental Visits		
Medication and Supplements		
Health Insurance		
Life Insurance		
Long-Term Care Insurance		
Health Club		
Total Health and Medical		

Financial	Current	In retirement
Income Taxes (estimated annual, divided by 12)		
Retirement Savings		
Emergency Savings		
Credit Card Payments		
Other Debt Payments (not including mortgage)		
Total Financial		

Transportation	Current	In retirement
Auto Payments		
Fuel		

Public Transit/Taxi Fares		
Repairs & Maintenance		
License & Registration		
Auto Insurance		
Total Transportation		

Family Care	Current	In retirement
Tuition & Education		
Childcare		
Eldercare		
Pets		
Total Family Care		

Discretionary	Current	In retirement
Media		
Entertainment		
Dining Out		
Gifts		
Hobbies		
Gadgets		
Charitable Donations & Philanthropy		
Travel & Vacation		
Total Discretionary		

Miscellaneous	Current	In retirement

Invest Now

Vacation Property		
Recreational Vehicles		
Total Discretionary		

Planned Purchases	Current	In retirement
New Car		
Furnace		
Roof		
Appliances		
Home Remodel		
Total Planned Purchases		

One-Time Expenses	Current	In retirement
Wedding		
Milestone Vacation		
Philanthropic Gift		
Second Home		

RV		
Total One-Time Expenses		

PEACE OF MIND CHECKLIST

Most of life's major transitions and experiences can be documented with a series of important legal documents. These include documentation for changing jobs, purchasing a home or vehicle, planning for retirement, or end-of-life decisions.

When a major life event occurs, especially a crisis, it can be difficult to find the essential items required to make decisions. Perhaps they are in a filing cabinet in the basement, in a safe deposit box at the bank, or stored in digital files in your computer. If you take time to properly organize your documents, you will be prepared when you need them most. Give yourself the gift of organization and preparation before unexpected circumstances arrive.

We have prepared a Peace of Mind Checklist as a simple tool for organizing the vital documents of your life. As you complete this checklist, consider sharing it as well with close family members, an attorney, accountant, and your financial advisor. This easy process may be one of the most valuable gifts you can give yourself—and your family—when you need it most.

Important Contacts	Name	Phone Number
Financial Advisor		
CPA/Accountant		
Insurance Agent		
Attorney		
Executor of Estate		

Emergency Information	Location
Birth Certificate	
Social Security Card	
Passport or Citizenship (Naturalization Papers)	
Driver's License (Number and Expiration Date)	
Marriage Certificate	
Pre-Nuptial Agreement	
Divorce/Separation Papers	
Adoption Papers	
Safe Deposit Box(es) and Keys	
Safe and Combination	
Living Will	
Durable Power of Attorney	

Invest Now

Financial Information	Location
Checking Account Statements	
Checks	
Savings Account Statements	
Credit Card and Account Statements	
Life Insurance Policy Documents	
Credit Union Account Books or Statements	

Financial Documents	Location
Mortgage Documents	
Rental and/or Lease Agreements	
Real Estate Deeds and/or Other Titles of Ownership	
Medical Records, Prescriptions, Plans, Bills	
Appraisals for any Valuable Items	
Trust Documents/Agreements	
Inventory of Valuable Items	
Buy/Sell or Partnership Agreements	
Deferred Compensation Agreements	
Federal/State Gift-Tax Returns	
Prior Years' Tax Returns	
Motor vehicle Title and/or Registration Papers	

186

Promissory Notes	
Outstanding Loans	
Pending Lawsuits or Legal Actions	

Investment Documents	Location
Brokerage Account Statements	
Mutual Fund Account Statements	
Annuity Account Statements	
Individual Retirement Plan Statements	
Company Retirement Plan Statements	
Company Benefits (deferred compensation)	
Stock Certificates (not held in an account)	
Bearer Bonds (not held in an account)	
Alternative Investment Documents (Including K-1s)	
Investment Club Documents/Records	
529 College Savings Plan Statements	
Online Securities Access Information	
Beneficiary Forms for IRA, 401(k), and other benefit plans	

Invest Now

Documents showing cost basis of securities owned or sold	

Insurance Documents	Location
Life Insurance Policy Documents	
Group Life Policies	
Health and Accident Insurance ID cards	
Variable Annuity or Fixed Annuity Statements	
Mortgage Insurance Policy	
Travel Insurance Policy	
Property and Casualty Policy Documents	
Veterans Administration Insurance Papers	
Beneficiary Forms for Insurance or Annuity Policies	
Long-term Care Insurance Policy	

Final Arrangements	Location
Information for Obituaries (Resume, life story, biography)	
Last Will and Testament*	
Military Discharge Papers**	
Burial Instructions	

Cemetery Plot Deed	
Pre-Paid Cremation Documents	
Funeral Home Preferences	
Charitable Donations Preference(s)	
Letter of Instruction from the Deceased to Executor	
Death Certificate (Multiple Copies)	
Phone Number/Address of County Surrogate Court	

*Wills should be stored in a fireproof safe at your home or in a lawyer's will safe. Do not store wills in a safe deposit box.

**Veterans receive a small stipend toward burial expenses

ACKNOWLEDGEMENTS:

I'd like to thank the following people:

Tricia Heyer, a New York Times Bestselling writer with her name tucked into the acknowledgements of dozens of books. She collaborates with authors all over the world, and she happens to live in my neighborhood, so the writing appointments were an easy commute. Tricia proved she is willing to learn anything for a book she's writing, and this project offered her a crash course in understanding investments and preparing for a financial future. What a perfect collaboration, as she knew the questions to ask to make the language simple for anyone learning this for the first time. The highest form of learning is teaching, and she met the challenge.

Greg Johnson, President and literary agent with WordServe Literary Agency. He is a wizard with words and a leader in the publishing industry. Greg walked me through the publishing process, helping the seed of an idea to morph into a book we can hold in our hands.

I'd like to thank my partners and clients at Cherry Creek Investment Advisors. This book is for you.

ABOUT THE AUTHOR

Sean Castle Co-founded Cherry Creek Investment Advisors, Inc. in 1994 with the goal to help people just like you cut through the media driven "noise" associated with investing in today's financial markets.

He's been utilizing common-sense and time proven strategies to help people achieve their individual financial goals for over 25 years. Having navigated clients and their investments through the 1987 stock market crash and the Financial Crisis of 2008, he brings valuable experience to each and every client relationship he has.

As he often tells clients, "In spite of apocalyptic predictions, the world hasn't ended and likely won't." In his 25 years he's never seen anyone make money by panicking.

Having worked in Washington, D.C., both in Congress and as a Presidential appointee at the U.S. Treasury Department, Mr. Castle brings a unique understanding and clarity to the political issues that so often contribute to the volatility and confusion in today's investment world.

A published author and former host of a Denver based radio talk show discussing the markets and financial planning issues, Mr. Castle also speaks at various industry conferences, university functions, and business gatherings.

Over the years, Mr. Castle has served on a variety of corporate, non-profit, and government Boards of Directors. He is a graduate of Colorado State University (Go Rams!) with a B.A. in Economics.

Married for over 33 years and father to a fantastic teenage daughter, Mr. Castle enjoys traveling, photography, and scuba diving. In particular, he loves diving with sharks and has dove with over 12 different species of sharks.

END NOTES

[1] Robert T. Kiyosaki, *Rich Dad, Poor Dad* (Scottsdale: Plata Publishing, Second Edition, 2017).

[2] Money Guy. (www.moneyguy.com)

[3] Kara McGuire, *The Teen Money Manual: A Guide to Cash, Credit, Spending, Saving, Work, Wealth, and More* (North Mankato: Capstone, 2015), 6.

[4] Kara McGuire, *The Teen Money Manual: A Guide to Cash, Credit, Spending, Saving, Work, Wealth, and More* (North Mankato: Capstone, 2015), 6.

[5] Robert Kiyosaki, *Rich Dad, Poor Dad.* (Scottsdale: Plata Publishing, Second Edition, 2017).

[6] Bankrate.com. Fewer Than 4 In 10 Americans Could Pay A Surprise $1,000 Expense From Savings, January 2021.

[7] Cherry Creek Investment Advisors, Inc.

[8] https://www.getrichslowly.org/

[9] Compounding: The Eighth Wonder of The World. TheNewSavvy.com, January 2016.

[10] Berkshire Hathaway Portfolio Tracker (cnbc.com). CNBC "Buffett Watch." Accessed March 4, 2022.

[11] 16 Money Rules That Millionaires Swear By, GOBankingRates.com, February 2022.

[12] 16 Money Rules That Millionaires Swear By, GOBankingRates.com, February 2022.

[13] What Exactly are the Points in the Dow Jones? (smartcapitalmind.com), May 8, 2022.

[14] What Is the Dow Jones? (Stock Market Indexes)

(investopedia.com)

[15] www.marketwatch.com

[16] What Exactly are the Points in the Dow Jones? (with picture) (smartcapitalmind.com), May 8, 2022.

[17] S&P 500® | S&P Dow Jones Indices (spglobal.com)

[18] What is the S&P 500 Index & How Do I Use It? (fool.com)

[19] How to Handle Stock Market Corrections (thebalance.com)

[20] Understanding Asset Allocation for Your Portfolio | The Motley Fool

[21] Correlation Definition (investopedia.com)

[22] Asset Class Definition (investopedia.com)

[23] Brinson, Singer, and Beehower, "Determinants of Portfolio Performance II: An Update." *The financial Analysts Journal,* 1991.

[24] What is a REIT (Real Estate Investment Trust)? | REIT.com

[25] The Benefits of Master Limited Partnerships (investopedia.com)

[26] Cryptocurrency Definition (investopedia.com)

[27] Rule of 72 Definition, Formula, & Calculation (investopedia.com)

[28] Investopedia, June 2015.

[29] How Much Did Things Cost in 1939? (reference.com)

[30] How Much It Costs To Buy A Gallon Of Milk In Each State – Zippia

[31] United States Average Hourly Wages | 1964-2021 Data | 2022-2023 Forecast | Historical (tradingeconomics.com)

[32] Ironman Blog | Median Household Income In April 2021 | Talkmarkets

[33] Fresh whole milk price history from 1939 through

2021 (in2013dollars.com)

[34] Hyperinflation Definition (investopedia.com)

[35] What is Liquidity and Why is Liquidity Important? (financialmodelingprep.com)

[36] Joshua Brown and Brian Portnoy, *How I Invest My Money: Finance Experts Reveal How they Save, Spend, and Invest* (Petersfield: Harriman House, 2020), 37.

[37] Appendix A.

[38] Matt Krantz, *Retirement Planning for Dummies* (Hoboken: John Wiley & Sons, 2020), 84.

[39] Larry Swedore and Kevin Grogan, *Your Complete Guide to a Successful & Secure Retirement* (Great Britain: Harriman House, 2019), 1.

[40] Products - Data Briefs - Number 427 - December 2021 (cdc.gov). Center for Disease Control and Prevention, National Center for Health Statistics, Mortality in the United States, 2020.

[41] Larry Swedore and Kevin Grogan, *Your Complete Guide to a Successful & Secure Retirement* (Great Britain: Harriman House, 2019), 5.

[42] Mark Lichtenfeld, *You Don't Have to Drive an Uber in Retirement: How to Maintain Your Lifestyle without Getting a Job or Cutting Corners* (Hoboken: John Wiley & Sons, 2018).

[43] Shelly Schwartz, "Most Americans, Rich or Not, Stressed About Money: Survey," *CNBC,* August 3, 2015, www.cnbc.com/2015/08/03/most-americans-rich-or-not-stressed-about-money-surveys.html.

[44] Eric Thurman, *Thrive in Retirement: Simple Secrets for Being Happy for the Rest of Your Life* (Colorado Springs: Waterbrook, 2019).

[45] Thurman, 160.

[46] NerdWallet, 2020 American Household Credit Card

Debt Study
[47] Kevin Rose, "The Latecomer's Guide to Crypto," in *The New York Times,* Sunday March 20 2022.

Made in USA - Kendallville, IN
47422_9781941555569
02.10.2023 1331